> *Mirror, mirror, on the wall,*
> *Who is the fairest of them all?*
> *– Brothers Grimm, "Snow White"*

Model: Jurata
Image: Mol Smith
Title: "Mirror, Mirror…"

ONVIEW BOOKS
I Wannabe A Model
Published by Onview.net Ltd
2009

Registered Office:
Onview.net Ltd., 4a Oxford Road, Wallington, Surrey. SM6 8SJ. England.

Distribution:
Frilford Mead, Kingston Road, Frilford. Abingdon. Oxfordshire. OX13 5NX England

www.iwannabeamodel.net

The moral right of the author has been asserted.
Many thanks to Lesley Evans for proof-reading my book.

First Published 2009 by (Onview Books) Onview.net Ltd.

A CIP catalogue record for this book is
Available from the British Library.
ISBN 978-0-9557137-1-2

I Wannabe A Model

A guide to being a successful female model through Internet promotion and modelling know-how.

By Mol Smith

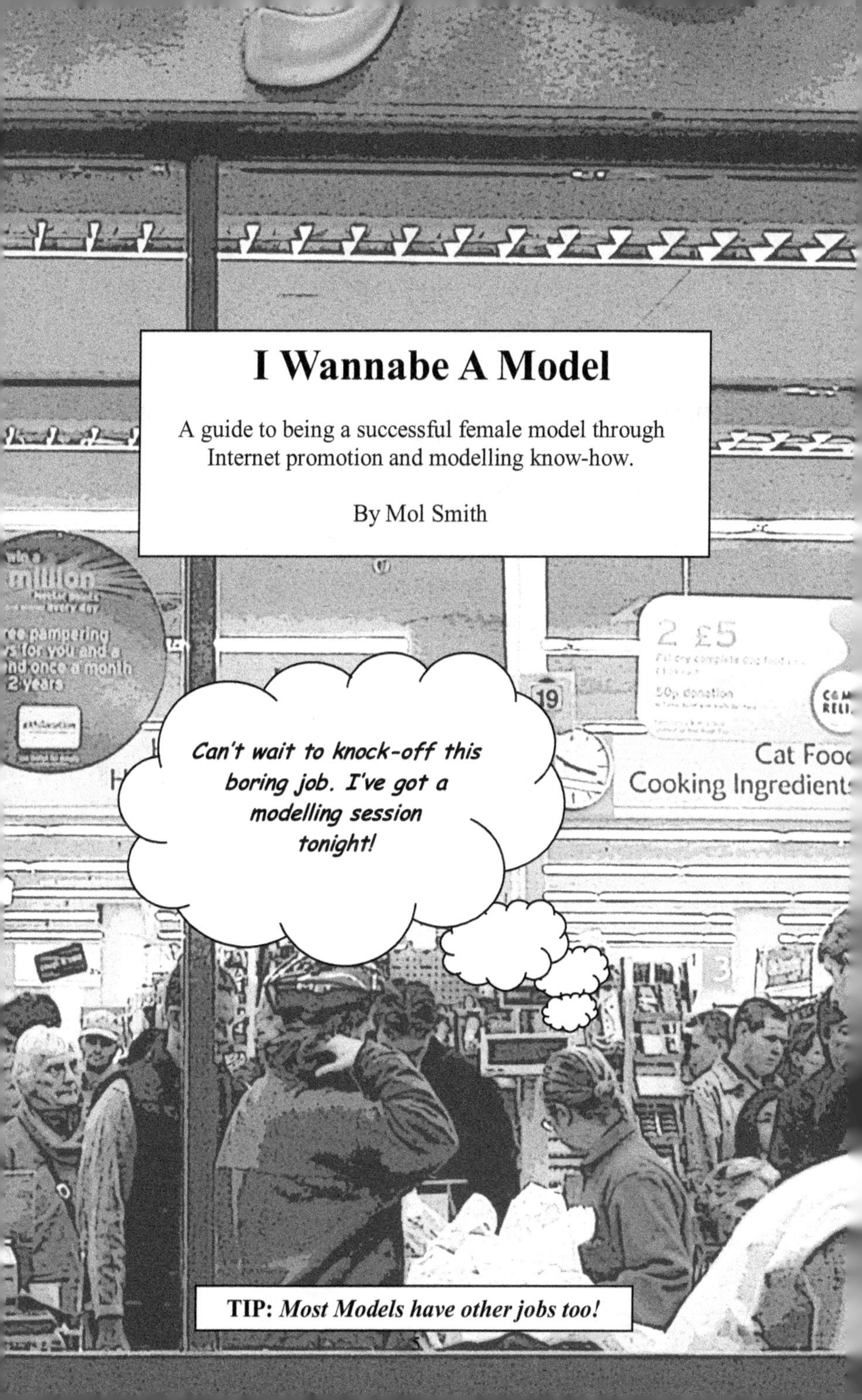

TIP: ***Most Models have other jobs too!***

Acknowledgements & Credits

I guess nothing is ever produced completely by oneself. People help in all kinds of ways both directly and indirectly. All images of models in this book have been credited below where I can remember their names. The following people are owed a special mention:

Lesley Evans—for putting up with me and my passions, but most of all for trying to remove all my clumsy mistakes here.

Kitten von Mew—for allowing me to publish her own images without pay.

My mum, now sadly gone to another place, for introducing me at a young and innocent age to the power of books and images.

Every female who made the effort to push themselves out of bed and come to work with me paid or unpaid, and for making it on time, and trusting me.

Mol

Model Picture Credits.

Model	Page
Abigail	91
Allison	34,91
Aimee	88
Angela	36
Beccy_G	42,43,44
Beth	12,14,27,35,53,54,55,56
Binur	98
Charlotte G	34
Chloe	70,71
Clair	20
Daisy	33
Eve	61,62,94,95
Grace	56
Helen	32
Ivana	16,19,56
Jenny	56,79-87
Johanne	55,56
Jurata	2,12,90
Kira Krueger	59
Kitten von Mew	40,41
Lenka	15
Lesley	7
Michelle	55,56
Rosaline	37
Rosanne	13
Sarah	91
Steph	88,89

You are all Stars!

Contents

Visit the web site:
www.iwannabeamodel.net

Many thanks Lesley, my muse, for your
work on this book. Love Mol xx

Introduction

Who is this book for?

Is it for you? Well, if you are a female aged between 15 to 55 and you wish to pose in front of a camera on a regular basis for whatever reason, then yes— it's for you. You may be just starting out, already modelling or considering becoming a model. It doesn't matter which, because I have attempted to contain all you need in this one little book.

Who am I?

You would probably think a book like this might be best written by a female model. You may be right but I am a **DIGITAL ARTIST**, male, and I have worked with hundreds of models just in the last 9 years. I have spoken with many of them about their paths into modelling and how they get work. I have seen women who have been relatively successful and those who gave up very quickly.

As a photographer and artist, I began my adventure into depicting women in art way back in time, and after giving it up for a while to rear children, I returned to it about 9 years ago. What you learn through this book is not just my experience and advice but that of other models I am in contact with.

A few quick tips on using this book

Any endeavour is littered with phrases, jargon, and abbreviations unknown to those starting out. Modelling is no different. Throughout the book, you will find all **STENCIL** text phrases explained in the Jargon Buster Section at the back of the book. I have tried to make the book interesting and I have tried to inspire you by including images and visual examples from my own work. The more you know about the photographic process as well as the modelling process, the better model you will be; so I have included material from a photographer's point of view as well.

You can flip through the book and dive into the bits you want to know, and that's okay; but as it is not a really hefty work, why not just carry on from here and work your way through. I have written it in a chatty, friendly, and hopefully humorous and witty style, not to seem clever, but to keep you involved. In fact, let's get something right straight away, I want you to become a great female model! That is part of my reason for writing this book. I mean, who knows, one of your first assignments after reading it all the way through might be here in my studio in front of my camera.

Now wouldn't that be great for both of us?

Mol

Chapter 1: Why be a model?

Women model for a variety of reasons, from wanting to be involved in a creative process through to wanting a highly paid modelling career. Most female models may even start out with a specific aim but determine through modelling that their intention and reasons change. I have met students attending university modelling to help pay their way through their courses, girls with routine jobs who model for fun and as an interest, and models bent on earning some real money from their talent and skill.

Many girls reaching the age of puberty long to appear in front of a camera and be admired for their attractiveness. So, let's quickly deal with that one. If you are under the age of eighteen, very few photographers will be interested in working with you because of your age. All good and morally correct photographers may consider working with you if at least one parent is with you throughout the entire process. I have done this with exceptionally attractive girls but only on 4 occasions in 9 years, and always with care about the type of image produced, and always with one or both parents with me in the studio at all times.

So if you are only 15, 16, or even 17, you may be old enough to know your own mind and be street-wise, and everything else, but without your parents absolute support you should not end up in front of a camera anywhere. Photographers who do offer you work, if you are below 18, without your parent's consent and presence may be good guys taking big legal risks, or bad guys out to exploit you... so be warned!

That said, let's consider the majority of women who wish to model or are already modelling. Our lifestyles in the west are determined greatly by the media, or at least our perceptions are. The world of fashion, as viewed through the glossy magazines, television, and cinema seems attractive, glamorous, and desirable. Female models adorn the covers of Vogue Magazine and drift before our eyes draped with gorgeous wealthy men. They are often in the best surroundings with seemingly stunning life-styles. But if you look carefully, you will discover most top models are under tremendous stress and often have break-downs or end up taking drugs in a hopeless attempt to sustain their hectic and high pressured work.

There are tens of thousands of models out there just in the UK and the USA alone. About 1 in 10,000 of them will ever evolve to be a top catwalk model. There are probably less photographers by an order of 100 to 1 and very few of them make any money from photographing females. So, here's the rub: if you aim to be a model thinking you will end up as another Kate Moss, the chances are almost every single time that you are going to be very, very disappointed. If 10,000 people are currently reading this book, only 1 of you (if any) will ever adorn the front page of Vogue Magazine and sustain a top class modelling career. I am not putting you off trying but I am doing my best to tell you the truth straight away. This does not mean you should not be a model: it means you should be realistic about your aims. First things first—if you have a full time job, keep it! Explore the world of modelling on a part-time basis first. The practical world of routine work may not be exciting and 'sexy' but it will keep you alive, pay the bills, and act as a safety net for you to explore modelling with very low risk. If you do find yourself snapped up by a top agency and you are being called out every other day to well-paid assignments, then you can consider chucking in the rat-race job for a few years and make a career in modelling.

Just in case my comments are still not making you wise, I have known stunning looking drop-dead gorgeous women who you think would have no trouble getting signed up to good agencies, yet this is what they got told:

"You are too old". *The girl was nineteen.*
"You are too short". *The girl was 5'11".*
"Knock a few pounds off and come back". *The girl was tall, slim, 20 years old and curvy.*

Discounting a desire to become a top world-class female model, let's look at other more realistic reasons. By doing this and understanding your starting point, what I have to say may help you tailor your activities to achieve your aims. See which one (or more) of the following best suit your desire to be a model:

1. I can't get a job at the moment and think it might give me some income.
2. I am at university or college and could model to help give me support money.
3. People tell me I should be a model, so I thought—why not?
4. I have a good job and fancy modelling as an interest (or) I just fancy adding a bit of spice to my life.
5. I have a job, but maybe modelling might add some money to my income.
6. I am involved in other art forms (acting) and have spells without work so modelling can provide financial support in between jobs.
7. I love art and just want to be involved in some way.
8. I want to model as an interesting and intriguing hobby.
9. I just arrived here and speak very little English, so modelling would be a great way of making some money.
10. I am resident abroad where wages are low and I can make a little more money by visiting the UK and getting modelling assignments.
11. I want to get involved in theatre or TV presentation, and I think modelling might help me to get into that line of work.
12. I want to get into movies, and this is one way of getting noticed.
13. Don't know. Just fancy it.
14. Other.

And now, having made the choice of which best describes your reason to be modelling right now or to try modelling, see what I think may help you first below. What I have to say is for the majority of people in each choice. It is important to remember there are exceptions.

I can't get a job at the moment and think it might give me some income.
Well it might but not straight away. Just like any activity, it takes experience, time, know-how, and planned intent to make a success of anything. You should not stop chasing other work, because getting into an income position and receiving even a small amount of money regularly, will take several months work. It may involve you spending money just to get to the starting point. You need images of yourself which present you well, and although there are ways of building up a portfolio without spending much, it will take time and possibly some money to get started. Later, I will explain how to build up your portfolio but if you want money right now, then get any job… and I mean *any job* to get money in and then see if you can build up a portfolio, gain modelling experience. and win assignments in your spare time.

I am at university or college and could model to help give me support money.
It can but you will still have to build up a portfolio so much of what applies above will also apply to you too. One of the issues you should also consider is this: unless your studies are involved with the arts in some way, will modelling ultimately affect your chosen career/ For example, suppose you are studying to be a Barrister or have a career in politics—where public opinion, traditional values, and the general public might frown on images of you re-appearing later in life, clad in glamour lingerie and looking very sexy. Ask yourself, "Will my modelling come back and haunt me later?"

If not, and you are certain… away you go. Modelling can give you an income but it will not be regular—unlike working behind a bar at night or doing a Saturday job. If you get it right though and you have a good look, shape, and outlook, you will get paid work, but you might need to be fairly comfortable with partial or full nudity. The fashion, catalogue, and advertising industries are oversubscribed with full time models wanting work. You will need to fit into a niche where models are required part-time, and mostly by photographers looking for a younger woman uninhibited by nudity, who will work for money less than that demanded by full time models in a similar frame of modelling genre.

People tell me I should be a model, so I thought—why not?
Maybe, think 'why?' instead. Many women can be flattered and conditioned into all kinds of false belief. Ask people who don't know you very well and see if they all think you have the looks and figure other people would love to see? If they all think—"wow", then maybe you can start to consider it, but what do you want out of it: money, fame, fun, a hobby, kudos? Look at the

list again once you know. I have met lots of models who were been told some nonsense from their boyfriends just to flatter them, so watch out.

I have a good job and fancy modelling as an interest (or) I just fancy adding a bit of spice to my life.
Bingo! You are likely not to be disappointed but there are pitfalls to watch out for. If you are prepared to work without pay in return for prints of yourself, lots of photographers will probably ask you to model for them. The prettier you look—the greater the opportunity to get asked! You still need to plan your way carefully and to set limits on the type of genre and degree of exposure you are prepared to model for. One thing to watch out for is to make sure you are not out of pocket. Always ask if you can have your travel

expenses paid. There are lots of other things you need to know. Let the rest of this book become your bible. Jurata and Beth, depicted above, just wanted to model for fun and interest. They had a great time, met each other, and to this day—have great images hanging on their walls at home as a memory of their experience.

"Christl! He's trying to put us off!"

"Nah..! He's trying to help us!"

12

I have a job but maybe modelling might add some money to my income.
It sounds like you don't really like your job. I think the things I said in the
reason just before this one will also apply to you.

**I am involved in other art forms (acting) and have spells without work so
modelling can provide financial support in between jobs.**
It can but not easily. You might do better than others because you are already
involved in the arts. You are probably more able to stand in front of a camera
and pose without feeling inhibited, possibly would see it as fun too. Maybe
you prefer to do this than reach for a mundane job until you get main stream
work for your line of art? At least it's closer to what you love. Make sure you
explain to the photographers you are from an art discipline and enjoy art
work. Many photographers and artists do not make money from what they do,
but they love to work with other creative people and understand quite readily
the problems with earning money in the art professions. These people, rather
than agencies, companies, and editorial photographers are most likely to rustle
up some pounds from their mainstream employment, pensions, whatever... to

pay you to work with them, and they will truly empathise with the issues today of funding art and artistes. Aim at the artists and plead poverty. If you like them as people, you will probably get a buzz out of their personalities too, so making a bit of 'get-through' money will be more fun than canvassing or marketing work.

I love art and just want to be involved in some way.
Double Bingo! You could end up as an artist's muse, an enviable position if you love art but you have not chosen a career path in one of the arts. The issue for you is to find an artist or photographer who you have synergy with and whom you can trust. The photographer or artist/muse relationship is special and can be rare yet rewarding in so many non-physical ways. Such

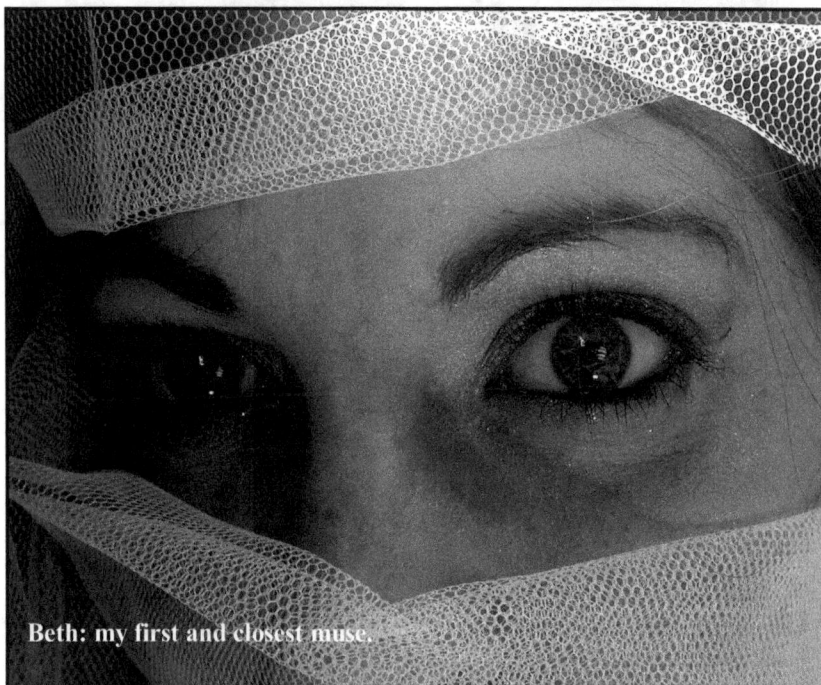

Beth: my first and closest muse.

relationships lead to extraordinary art, introspection, and joy. I have created my best art through artistic relationships with several muses, and what we have created together is extraordinary. A muse/artist relationship is so rare that most artists/photographers and models never find their respective muse. If you do and are certain about it, you are in for the greatest art joy of all, and something that most people on the planet never experience. It is not about you and him/her: it is about something called creativity and passion—focused into a unity unlike anything else in human relationships. It is not a physical relationship, but a spiritual one… or something close to this.

I want to model as an interesting and intriguing hobby.

You will not be disappointed. Many women model as a hobby. They meet all kinds of artistic people and often travel to other countries in pursuit of being photographed by a well-sought-after photographer. You also end up with lots of interesting images of yourself, and you will have a hobby with a degree of kudos that is quite different from other people.

I just arrived here and speak very little English, so modelling would be a great way of making some money.

It would be if you spend time and money to get yourself a great portfolio, market yourself, and you look good. Some women from eastern Europe do just that but in most cases they tend to meet someone who helps them. Lenka, pictured below, was a model of this ilk. Finding modelling work still requires

a basic skill of language and there are many good female models already who can speak English well. You will be competing against them for work. If you are attractive and you have an eastern European look, you will find it easier as many photographers like to photograph women of different cultures. However, if you are looking urgently for any quick-paid work, it might be best if you went to an agency specialising in employment for non-English-speaking people. Invariably, this type of work will be domestic work like cleaning, but it would give you a small living wage regularly and thereby enable you to explore modelling part-time as a way to increase your income.

I am resident abroad where wages are low and I can make a little more money by visiting the UK and getting modelling assignments.

Quite a few models from eastern European countries find cheap flights to the UK and zip over for a few days modelling work. In most cases, their modelling will involve a degree of nudity. They often charge less than their English counterparts, but recent changes in the value of the pound against the Euro, coupled with growing economies in their own countries, has undermined their potential to win work by charging less. However, if you are in this category of wanting to model, many photographers quite like the eastern European look, and find the variety of cultural differences in western appearances as an appealing facet.

A good idea you might consider is something done by two models I know—Ivanka in Slovakia, and Oksana in the Ukraine. As they have travelled to the UK to model many times, they have become experienced in this area of work sufficiently to understand the demand of photographers looking for women uninhibited by nudity. Both models have independently set up small loosely organised agencies in their own countries. They help other women find modelling work abroad, and also arrange package trips for photographers to visit

Oksana

Ivanka

their countries to work with local models relatively cheaply. If you can speak English well, you can act as an interpreter between the photographer and the other models, who may have no command of English at all.

You could speak with local hotel owners and restaurants about special pricing for groups and thereby set up good deals for photographers to come and stay for a few days to photograph models on your books. As you will know the surrounding environment well, you can also recommend outdoor locations to shoot at as well as finding a studio location for internal shoots.

I want to get involved in theatre, or TV presentation, and I think modelling might help me to get into that line of work.
I doubt it to be honest. You would do better to try directly for the type of work you really wish to do. You might like to try modelling as a way of getting used to being in front of a camera or to overcome any inherent shyness, but modelling alone is not going to open up acting careers for most people. Often it works the other way round, where people involved with the acting profession do some modelling between jobs to supplement their income.

I want to get into movies and this is one way of getting noticed.
I think you should read my advice above as it is probably valid for you too.

Don't know. Just fancy it.
If you 'fancy it' as an interest or hobby, all well and good. Try it and see if you enjoy it. If you 'fancy it' as a job, you should consider it no less a endeavour to that of doing any other job. It can be tiring, stressful, hard work—just like many other demanding jobs but if you're up for that, then sure...why not see how you get on.

Other
Did I miss something? I can't think of any other reason, but I would love to hear it if you have one.

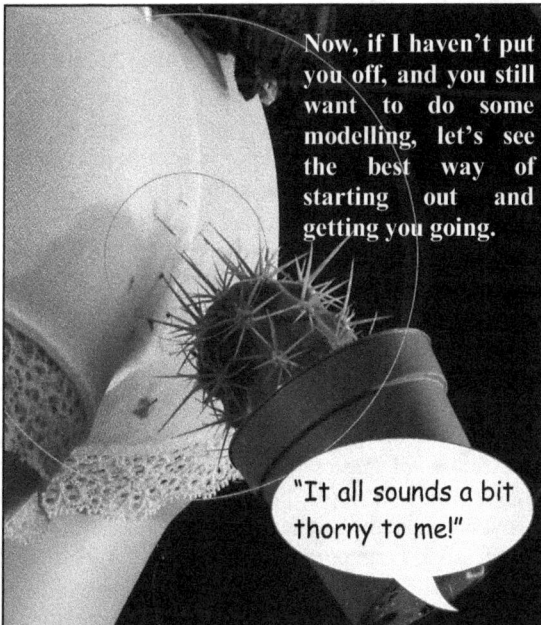

Now, if I haven't put you off, and you still want to do some modelling, let's see the best way of starting out and getting you going.

"It all sounds a bit thorny to me!"

Chapter 2: Starting Out

No matter which type of female modelling you are aiming to do—there are various genres, which I will go through shortly—you are going to need a **PORTFOLIO** of photographs. Years ago, this would have been achieved by going to a high street photographer, or via contact with an agency—to a specialist photographer, and paying up to £750 for a set of glossy prints. Some people still, unwisely, go down that route but I strongly recommend you don't go that way.

The Internet has changed many ways of doing things. There are web sites now which allow a model to gain access to photographers prepared to photograph you for free, or nearly free, as the deal will be they give you prints or a CD containing prints in return for you modelling for them. All you need to do is to get a friend to take a few head and body shots of you, and then load a few of these onto a model portfolio site saying you are a newbie prepared to work in exchange for prints or CD, in order to get photographers to see if they would like to work with you without anyone paying out money. There are some extra things to consider, of course, and I will go through these in a moment, but this is almost certainly the best way to start out. The only exception to this is if you try an agency out and they are so wowed by you that they want to snap you up straight away. Unlikely! But if they do, you should not have to part with any money—not for sign-up, photos, or anything else. If the agency asks you for money, forget the deal. Why should you be paying for anything if they think you are so hot that they want to sign you up and get you work?

Getting your very first photos
Please, please, don't snap yourself with your mobile phone and use these on a portfolio site. They create the worse impression of you, more than you imagine. Most people have cameras, if not you, then a friend. A digital camera is a must! You need about six really good shots of you. Photographers have thousands of pounds worth of equipment, including cameras, assorted lights, fans, backdrops, rigs, props, light meters and special light-firing devices to help them achieve excellent photographs. Unless you have a photographer as a friend (not a bad idea to find one to befriend), you will not have the quality of camera or equipment let alone the knowledge to take brilliant photos of yourself. But with a little advice from me, you can get those all-important first six photos onto a web site portfolio to kick off access to improved photos of yourself by professional or semi-professional photographers. First and foremost, plan some time with a friend to take a set of photos of you, and treat the moment as seriously as you would a real photo-shoot with a professional photographer. You should reserve a whole afternoon for this activity. Most digital cameras have flash guns. The problem is they are not suited for proper image capture of people in a flattering way. So the

best advice I can give is: turn the flash off! Most cameras of any real worth have manual settings where you can disable the flash-light. Please do this or tell your friend to do it. You are going to use natural light only to illuminate yourself. One way of doing this is to stand close to a window that has lots of light coming in. You should get your friend with the camera to stand to the side of you, and turn your head slightly towards him, so that light from the window is falling on at least half your face, or better still—two thirds. If you have a second friend present, you can ask him or her to hold a large mirror out of shot to reflect light from the window onto the darker side of your face and body. Alternatively, you can do the whole shoot outside in the garden or in a local park maybe.

Example: see text.

Ivana, photographed in natural light and un-touched .

The best light conditions are on those days which are slightly over clouded. Most flipping days in England seem to be like that today so it should not be hard. Avoid bright hot sunny days like the plague because such lighting conditions are likely to over brighten parts of you and completely blacken out other parts in shadow. Your friend must hold the camera very still. When not using the flash, a camera opens it's shutter for a longer time, and any slight movement, even the photographer breathing is likely to blur the image. Maybe s/he can rest the camera on a table or some other object for some of the shots to help steady it? Your friend must press the button very gently so as not to cause the camera to move. Most digital cameras focus as you press the button halfway down and then take the picture as the button is fully depressed. Make sure your friend knows this, and watch them do it to ensure they are waiting for the camera to auto-focus before depressing the button fully and taking the shot. You should decide before-hand what you are going to wear, how you are going to arrange your hair, and you should do your own makeup. Spend the time to get the best job done on this aspect. Think of doing several changes of clothes and hair styles so that each of your six photos are not all the same. Probably you should aim at six pictures as follows:

- A good head shot with a hint of a smile or full smile
- A full body shot showing your legs and entire frame

- One with you in a dress.
- If you intend to do more revealing modelling, one of you in lingerie.
- If you do not intend to model for anything revealing, dress in top and skirt. High heels lift you up if you are not very tall.
- One with you not looking at the camera, maybe instead— peering out of the window, or looking at something just above and to the right of the photographer's head.
- One of you sitting down. Kitchen stools are good for this as you can angle your legs out and make them look longer. Outside, you may find a wall, steps, or something similar to sit on.

Tell your friend to take several shots of each pose. Try not to blink when s/he fires the camera. Try different expressions. After each set of shots, go through them by playing them back on the camera's viewing screen to see how they look, and shoot them again if you can see things which can be improved on.

Here are a few tips:

- If possible, try to pose with a plain uncluttered background.
- A plain wall outside is often better than a busy street.

- Make sure your headshot is two-thirds turned, so you see both your face front and part side. The image on the left of Claudette shows what a two-thirds shot looks like. Notice you can see Claudette's face front and side.
- Open your eyes a little more than normal, but not so much that you are obviously doing it.
- Try a different expression for each 2 or 3 shots.

- Wear skirts and dresses, not trousers!
- Don't hide yourself behind your hair. If you have long hair, do some shots with your hair down and some with your hair up. Photographers want to see your face and bone structure as well as the shape of your body.
- Even if you are going to model in a more revealing genre, do not pose nude in your first six shots. Wear something semi see-through instead, or lingerie which covers your pubis and nipples: portfolio sites often will not show your photos free if they are more suitable for adults, and you need to expose your first pictures to as wide an audience possible without restrictions.
- Don't expect these photos to be comparable to a professional photographer's work. They wont be but they will suffice for now.

Preparing your photos to be printed

The photo in the digital camera needs to be put onto a computer. Most cameras have support for this which usually means plugging in a cord between the camera and the computer, and then using the camera's software to perform the transfer. I see no need to explain this task here as the camera will have directions on how to do that. What we do need to discuss though is image size and **DPI.** You also need to understand what a **TIFF** image is and what a **JPG** image is. When the image comes from the camera onto the computer, it may be a file known as a {something}. jpg or a {something}.tif

A {something}.tif file is an image format file which does not corrupt the image each time it is opened and saved. It is a large file and is not suitable for emailing or putting directly on a web site. However, it is the best format for storing images on your computer as it keeps your image perfect. The other file format, a {something}.jpg is the right file format for images to be loaded onto web sites or to attach to emails. It is very special! When you save an image as a {something}. jpg, the image or photo is analysed by the image software being used, and its information is compressed massively so the file is nowhere as big as the equivalent one in a {something}.tif format. The only problem is that if you open it in an image editor and save it again, it will lose clarity each time you do it. The reason for this is the image is reanalysed and averaged out each time. After saving it just a few times with an image editor, the picture will become useless, and you will start to see small artefacts appearing in the image.

If your images come out of the camera and onto the computer in .jpg format, it is best to open each one with a image file editor and save a copy of it as a .tif file. This way, you can be sure you retain the original image. People like myself, who edit and clean up images, can open that tif file, edit it, clean up the image, and save it as a jpg file for you to use on the internet. It can also be saved as another .tif file for safe keeping, preferably with a different name—for example— {somethingA}.tif so as not to overwrite the original file.

Photo-editing software can be very expensive. Photographers use Adobe Photoshop, which costs over £600.00 but you do not need such powerful software, and you can get cheap yet effective image editors for about £9.95 from the internet. See my footnotes at the end of this chapter! The .jpg files that came out of the camera, which hopefully are transferred to your pc, in most cases will be .jpg files. If you try to print these out on your colour printer without doing a bit of magic on them, you will find they are far too big to fit on the A4 paper. All images for the internet and those in your camera are made up of files with a width value, a length or height value, and something called DPI, which stands for Dots Per Inch. This 'Dots Per Inch' thing is a critical issue, and it is something which confuses everyone, even me after all these years. All you need to understand initially is this: images must be 72 Dots per Inch (DPI) for the internet, emails, and the web, and 300 Dots per Inch (DPI) for printing out in the real world.

An image editor has functionality for you to resize an image. In Photoshop, the editor of choice for photographers, the resizing allows you to change the dpi of the image too. To prepare photos for printing, you need to change any 72 DPI photos into 300 DPI images first. This is how it is done in **PHOTOSHOP**. Your image editor will have a similar way of doing this.

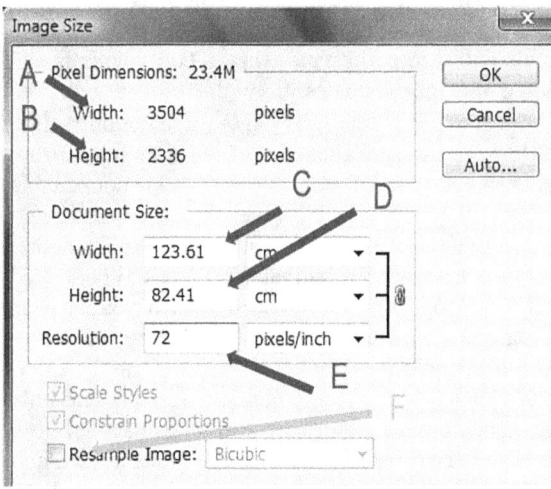

Here is a screen-shot from my Adobe Photoshop editor. This is the small window I get when I select 'resize image'.

You can see {E} the resolution is 72 dpi. The real pixel value width and height {A} and {B} are shown, and refer only to the size of the image when displayed full size on my screen. The monitor is made of tiny cells called pixels. Most modern monitors will be around 1440 x 900 pixels (that's width by height), so you can see if I showed an image of 3504 pixels wide by 2336 pixels high on my screen, it will be too big to see it all in one go. The important thing here is {C} AND {D}, as these values in centimetres will determine how big the image will print onto paper! The other thing is {E}, the DPI. We will never print an image set at 72 DPI , such values are only needed for images posted on the internet web sites, and sent in emails. We need to change the value in that box to become 300 DPI, like I have done here below. {F}, the 'resample image' tick-box, must **not** be checked! The picture, left, shows the same window after I enter 300 into the 'resolution' entry box.

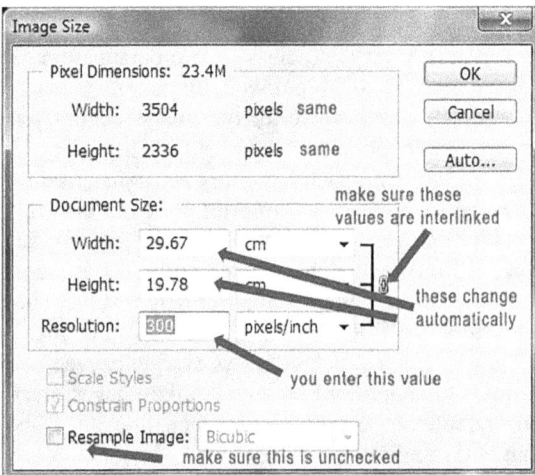

The width and height values are interlinked, which is what we always maintain to ensure any changes to the height or width is also done proportionally to the other dimension or side. But notice what changes. Look carefully. Do you see it? The real document size changes—both the width and the height. This is the size the image will be printed at on paper at 300 DPI: much smaller than when the image was set at 72DPI. The point here is this: *images printed at 72DPI will look all dotty, even though they may print larger. Images which are to be printed as photographs must have a minimum value 0f 300 DPI, no matter what the reduction in size is!*

Let's just recap a moment. What I have explained is how to prepare your images for printing. If you want to load them onto a portfolio web site (*yes, you do!),* a less complicated process is involved. Also, if you take the images from your camera and transfer them to a CD, or take the memory card out of the camera, and put either of these into of those photo-printing machines found everywhere now, the machine will sort out this whole DPI image size for you and simply print the photos as they should be. Not so bad then after all! It is a good ideas to understand all this techie stuff though, because when you work with your first photographers on a trade-off basis, both of your time traded with no money changing hands, *you want them to give you copies of the full sized images. You do not want them to give you just web-ready images because you will never be able to print them out as real photographs!*

Preparing your photos to go on the Internet (web portfolio sites).
I hope I didn't confuse you too much with this image sizing stuff. However, you are going to need to understand how to put your images onto the web. And they will always be set to a DPI size of.... what? Do you recall from the notes above and on the previous pages? Let me remind you: *web images are always 72 DPI, or more recently: 96 DPI. NOTE: I always use 72 DPI, but 96 DPI is also acceptable on most sites.*

Most web sites offering an opportunity to load a small portfolio, for free, restrict the number of images you can load and their size! You can't just take an image from your camera, even if it is already in the default DPI of 72, and whack it up onto a web site. It will simply be too large. You will need to make another file as a copy of the original and resize it so that it's width and height in pixels will be much smaller. A good starting size for web images is 800 pixels on the longest size. So long as you ensure the other side is set to change proportionally to the longest size in your image editor, you don't have to worry about that pixel value: you change one side, the other changes by itself! **Rather than demonstrate how to resize your pictures in Photoshop, I am** going to show you how to do it in a completely free image editor. You need to obtain a copy first. Here is the web address for the download:

http://www.getpaint.net/

So get on line and type it in your browser. Follow the links and messages to the download.

Once you have the download on your pc, use windows to unzip the file and extract the .exe program file to your disc drive. Locate and double click it to install it on your PC. I am not allowed to load the program file on my own server to make the download and installation simple for you, so if you have trouble installing it, please seek some help from a friend. Remember, right now at the time of writing, this software editor is FREE and it will help you resize you photo image files ready to put onto internet/web portfolio sites.

Here's how to do it.

Start the software.
Click on the top menu item 'file'
A drop down box appears.

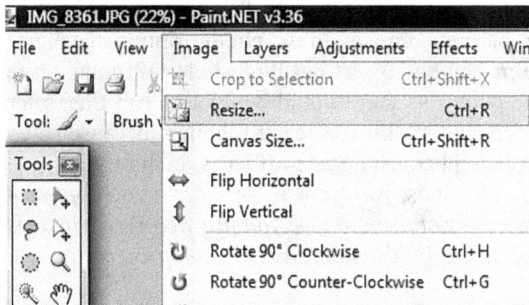

Click on 'open'
Locate and highlight the photo-image .jpg file you wish to resize.

Click 'Ok.'
When the file opens, locate and click on 'Image' in the editor's top menu.

A drop down box opens!

Select and click on 'resize' (See above)

You should get a window like this one on the right. Make sure all the settings are the same as mine for the red arrows. (*These are my arrows. You won't see them in your resize window*). If the Resolution is not 72 (see blue arrow), enter 72 in the box.

Good. You are now ready to resize the image to put on the web!

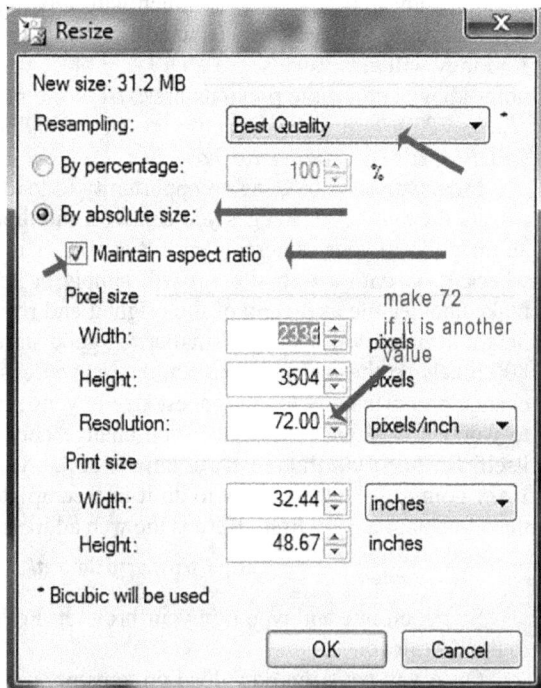

Whichever has the longest side in pixels, width or height, enter the figure 800 and click OK. That's it. Now save the file BUT select 'save as' from the menu and rename the file by adding a hyphen and the word 'web' in the file name. See below! This is so you don't over-write the original and you know which one is your web –ready file! Don't forget to work through your chosen photos ready to start your first online portfolio and begin the adventure into modelling.

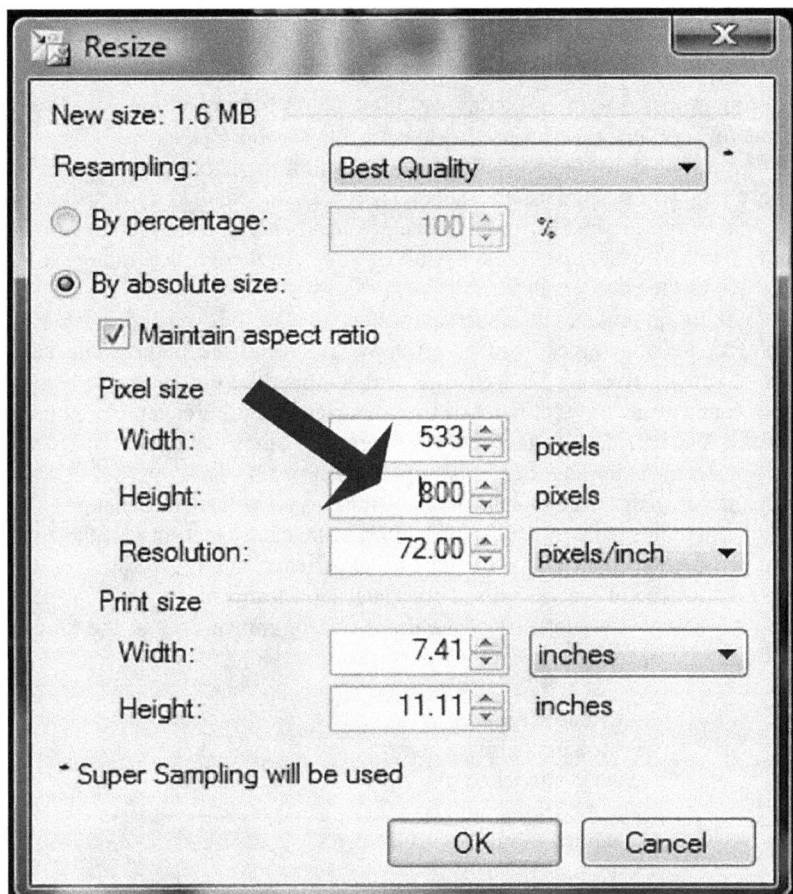

Resize

New size: 1.6 MB

Resampling: Best Quality

○ By percentage: 100 %

◉ By absolute size:

☑ Maintain aspect ratio

Pixel size

Width: 533 pixels

Height: 800 pixels

Resolution: 72.00 pixels/inch

Print size

Width: 7.41 inches

Height: 11.11 inches

* Super Sampling will be used

OK   Cancel

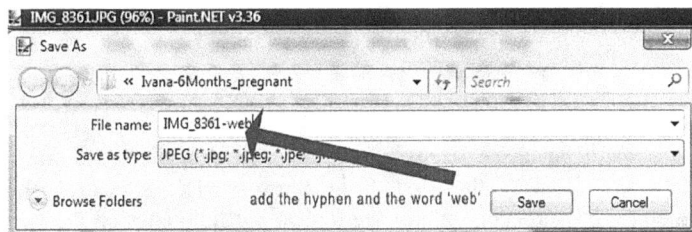

IMG_8361.JPG (96%) - Paint.NET v3.36

Save As

« Ivana-6Months_pregnant   Search

File name: IMG_8361-web

Save as type: JPEG (*.jpg; *.jpeg; *.jpe; *.jp...

Browse Folders   add the hyphen and the word 'web'   Save   Cancel

Registering with a Web Portfolio Site

In the past decade, the evolution of the Internet has led to the creation of Model Portfolio Sites where both Photographers and models can display their work to the public and other members of the site. It is by loading some of your photos onto one or more of these sites, that you will attempt to find good photographers to work with you in the future to help you build up your portfolio of images. Initially, because your number of photos are small and as you are just starting out, it is unlikely you will be offered payment for modelling. What you should do is attempt to find photographers prepared to photograph you on what is called a **TFP** basis. Time For Prints has become a bit of an outdated term and today we often use **TF*** to stand for a variety of 'Time for' options: time for prints, time for images on a CD, etc.

You give your time freely to model, and in return the photographer gives his time along with copies of the shoot on a CD, or emailed to you, or/and physical prints to you. No money changes hands but you may often ask for (and be given) your travel costs or half of your travel costs depending on the goodwill of the photographer.

It is important to understand that in the UK and the USA, a photographer automatically owns all copyright to all the photos s/he takes even if you are working for free. This is determined by statute law in both of these countries along with most of the countries in the European Community as well. We will discuss the entire arrangement along with your rights and best practice, regarding the shooting session itself, later on but for the moment, we wish to get your portfolio on-line so we will stick to that.

There are many portfolio web sites, with more emerging all the time. Some of them specialise. As you pick up experience and know-how, you can investigate some of the specialised ones later on. Meanwhil

e, below is a short list of the more widely known ones at the time of writing.

www.musecube.com
www.onemodelplace.com
www.net-model.com
www.modelmayhem.com
www.purestorm.com
www.modelplace.com
www.starnow.co.uk
www.allmodelzone.com
www.modelcruz.com
www.newfaces.com
www.gothicmodels.net

I haven't put these is any particular order except for the fact I have portfolios myself with the first 5 in the list. The site near the top, onemodelplace, is probably one of the largest portfolio sites on the web with somewhere in the region of 122,079 models having portfolios there, and over 37,000 photographers or somewhere in that order of magnitude. As it is a large site, it might be best if you are just starting out to put your portfolio on the smaller sites like net-model or model-mayhem. These have a large number of portfolios too but not nearly as many, as far as I can tell, as onemodelplace.

Each site generally allows models to put up a small number of photographs for free. They hope you will be successful enough in getting work from photographers to want to expand your portfolio and load many more higher quality images. A small charge is made monthly by subscription if you wish to do this later. Further advantages in competing for work are offered to you via a range of subscription options, prices, and functionality on each site. You should take note that you can have portfolios on many sites and not just on one alone. You can also create your very own web site but this is not needed unless you become quite engaged in modelling. I have included some advice about having your own web site later in this book.

When you register on a portfolio site, it is best to use an alias name, that is—a made-up one. This gives you a degree of privacy and safety. Not everyone visiting modelling sites are professional people, so without getting too hung-up about it, you must always take measures to safeguard yourself. Good model portfolio sites will protect your privacy: people will only be able to email you via the site, and you reply back to them via the site too, not from your personal email address directly. Later on as you get to know your way around a bit, you will get a feel for who is safe and who is not (most are perfectly safe). Until then, always think of

privacy and safety first and make it a good idea to maintain these aspects even when you do become far more experienced. 'Safety First' is a good rule, and the right kind of photographers will respect and understand it!

All age groups	Models of 18 years or older
Print/Editorial	Lingerie
Runway	See-through
Fashion	Glamour
Sport/Fitness	Implied Nude
Casual / Catalogue	Topless
Swimwear/Bikini	Art Nude
Hair	Nude
Parts Modelling	Erotic Nude
Fine Art	Fetish
Alternative	Adult Nude
Artists Model	Pink

You will need to enter a lot of details about yourself including your email address. A lot of these details are made public but not your email address, which is normally kept private unless you click a box saying you want it made public. You don't! One of the things you will need to do is to say which genres of modelling you wish to work in. In case you are not familiar with the various genres, I will talk about them here now. You should read this before you sign-up to present a portfolio on a web site! The various modelling areas are listed below, followed by an explanation of each one.

Print/Editorial
This type of modelling, although suitable for all models and age groups, is appropriate and suitable for models who may not fit the classic notion of real beauty. Not all models can look fantastic, slim, or have the preferred shape, size, height, and 'look' of whatever is considered by a culture and its era, as stunning beauty. Women of all ages, shapes, and sizes are used as character models to portray ordinary people in catalogues, prints, magazines, newspapers, commercials, etc.,

Runway or Catwalk
In the USA, what Europeans call Catwalk Model, is termed Runway model. This might seem obvious to some but when I restarted as a photographer about 9 years ago, I was convinced there was this special genre in the States where models posed on military aircraft runways! I just naively thought this kind of photo-depiction was something with a narrow appeal to the armed forces. See where a little bit of innocence leads?

We all know what a Catwalk Model does. She models fashionable clothes, not just high fashion, but for chains of shops, stores, and mass shopper outlets. In the main, most catwalk models are a special breed: tall, elegant, with striking looks, or plain looks which can be easily altered to many different looks by a make-up artist. She will be at least 5'9", slim, and leggy.

Fashion
The main difference between fashion modelling and most of the other genres, lower down in my list above, is that fashion modelling focuses on the beauty of the clothes and not the model herself! She is the non-expressive walking prop, an 'ornament' enhancing the beauty of the outfit. High end fashion will require the model to look like the perfect woman. She will be at least 5'9", slim, and leggy.

Sports/Fitness
As the name suggests, sports and fitness modelling relies upon the model having a fairly athletic body and toned physique. Although not as heavily endowed with muscles as body-builders, except in exceptional areas of this genre, the model's muscle size is not so important as their ratio of body fat to overall body mass: the result of swapping body fat mass for muscle mass. If you do not have that kind of body and you don't 'work-out' on a regular basis, it is unlikely you will be suitable for this genre just through natural form and serendipity.

Casual Modelling / Catalogue
This opens up many opportunities for the models too short or not slim enough for high end fashion modelling. The requirement is for catalogues to sell clothes to a variety of women of different shapes and sizes. The model should be considered pretty and will represent the girl next door or the mature woman.

Swimwear/Bikini
This one is very obvious. Commercially, the model needs to have a physique closer to the fitness model as she is going

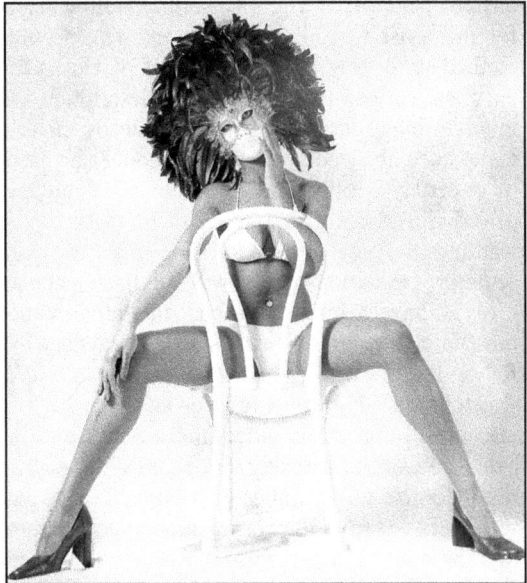

to be used to wear and market bikini and swimwear. She can be shorter than a fashion model: five foot, five inches is quite normal. Non-commercially, bikini models form a loose, less scintillating, version of glamour and pin-up modelling, where more of the model's body is shown than in fashion modelling. This constitutes a very mild form of titillation, quite harmless and acceptable in western cultures and societies. Most models below the age of 35 and sometimes much older, would have little problem with modelling bikini wear either commercially, or for a mild form of pin-up. The symmetry and clarity of a woman's form especially when she is close to the era's culture idea of beauty, is considered pleasing and not sleazy to most people. Models below the age of 18 may also do commercial bikini modelling.

Hair or Parts Modelling
Fairly obvious. Do you have great hair, pretty feet, wow-stocking-hugging legs, large-melt-them-down eyes? You do? Then determine what part of you is fantastic compared to ordinary women and market it well.

Fine Art / Artists Model
There is no real distinction between Fine Art and Artist's model. In the old days of pencil drawing, oil painting, and water colours, a model would pose for the artist to capture a likeness. This would normally be clothed, part-clothed, or a very graceful form of part or full nudity. This niche may still exist and serve a real purpose and description for those original ideas. It will involve long periods of careful steady position posing. From my own experience, the traditional artist's model role has leapt from the canvas and oil of yesterday into the now of digital paint and special effects under the talents of a digital artist. There may still be work in colleges for the fine art model wanting to pose for pencil and ink (or paint) drawings, and certainly sculptures in various guises will still have a demand.

I have a lot to say about this area of modelling partly because I am most interested in the Artist's Model category of model. The current demand for models to work with **DIGITAL ARTISTS** increases all the time. Look at the way our world is moving ever-faster towards a digital variant of special-effects still-image and video-image platform. The modelling world has yet to catch-up with its phrasing and peoples ideas of what a modern artist actually does! Expect to act rather than pose. Expect unusual propositions and ideas way-different from the normal modelling session. You could be a character in a graphic novel, a person interacting with objects and creatures not yet there in the studio with you. Digital artists are the future. They know photography,

The image on the opposite page demonstrates the type of image that can be created by a modern artist: a digital artist. The model posing for this was told roughly what the final image would look like. After the photo was taken, many hours were spent by the artist (little old me) to transform her into this mix of half flesh/half machine living entity, receiving unfair and cruel treatment in a futuristic world.

computer technologies, 3d modelling technologies, publishing technologies, video-making and editing, graphic-design, Anime techniques and more. The most exciting area of work is always in this genre. Sometimes it will be commercial: other times it will be for individuals like myself, interested in exploring these modern techniques without the restrictive practices imposed on them by commercialism. Some work will require nude or semi nude work. Make it clear in your portfolio information if you are okay about that or not.

Helen by mol

Alternative

Many forms of contemporary depiction of women no-longer fit into the time-honoured categories established back in the 1950's and 1960's for female modelling work. An alternative model may carry out modelling work that does not fit easily or completely into one of the traditional genres. Most of the advance of this new and exciting art-form and modelling niche, which has now entered the main-stream in movies and magazines, is accredited to the pioneering publishers 'Goliath' in Germany and 'Skin' magazine. The current set of sub-categories in this genre are: Punk, Goth (or Gothic), Tattooed, Fetish, and new less well-known and finer divisions. Make no mistake though, this area of modelling is as important as the more traditional ones, with a growing demand for the 'new' against the 'old seemed-to-be-tired' areas. Young people, emerging from the current generation of teenagers, see the world anew, and the next 50 years belongs to them, not the owners of the magazines, media, and the web-sites of today.

So if you are one of those people who wishes to take your fashion style into the world of modelling, believe in yourself and push it hard. You are the future! A good place for alternative models to find work is on a web site called 'Starnow'. The address: http://www.starnow.co.uk/

You may be able to pick up small crowd parts (probably unpaid, except for a sandwich and coffee) in one of those horror movies where loads of exotically dressed punks, Goths, Vamps, and other great looking people are hanging out in the Vampire night-club.

Lingerie, See-through, Glamour, Implied Nude, Topless

Each of these areas of modelling have slightly different aims and demands. I've grouped them together because they share a single thing in common: "sensuality & sexuality". A lingerie model will be expected to be okay with her breasts and pubic areas covered, yet she will often be viewed by the public as an arousing woman, half-clad, wearing little more than bra and panties, suspenders, stockings, hold-ups etc. In traditional terms, such imagery may simply fall into an aspect of fashion clothes modelling, or catalogue modelling. However, there is an overlap between the nature of scantily dressed females (or males) posing non-suggestively for basic display of clothes, and the scantily-dressed female who is the focus of the image *instead* of the clothes! So 'lingerie' to a photographer, means the model will willingly and comfortably be photographed in little more than underwear no-matter what the subject nature of the girl-alone pose.

See-through and Glamour is much like the old fashioned 'pin-up' but with fresh approaches and ever-more sensual connotation in a modern age. The western world long cast off its 1950's naivety !

You would not be expected to expose your nipples or your pubic hair, or more, in the strict realm of traditional glamour. But 'see-through' will mean parts of these more-private areas can be glimpsed in the resulting photograph. Flimsy clothes or outfits made from netting material can permit see-through! A model can be posed in such a way that the camera lens can visually probe between the loose fabric of a top or blouse and find the breast it is loosely covering. If you don't wear a bra but wear a wet top, or you wear a thong and you have pubic hair, the camera and the photographer wanting to shoot see-through expect to be able to record these details. Implied nude, in the main, means exposing your breast and sometimes—nipples, but nothing

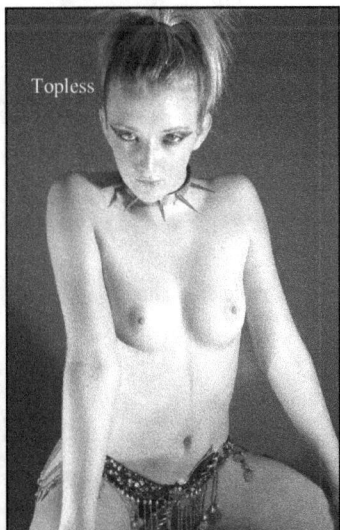

Topless

else. The idea is that in the photograph you will appear as if you were nude, but the observer of the final image will not see your vagina or pubic area. This is accomplished by a variety of 'devices' - maybe a draped piece of clothing over the 'sensitive' area; or the model can be turned and posed in such a way that the vaginal 'line' is not visible nor the pubic hair. There are variations on this: a model could be completely unclothed, but cover her breasts with her hands, bend her body, and pose her legs so that nothing of her sexual areas is captured on camera. All well and good but the photographer will see you! As long as you understand this, and the photographer is not clicking the camera until you are in the pose, your good self should not appear in the public arena with any vital

33

part of your sexual (and intimate) self on-show. Topless is quite close. It is the same as wearing no bra, but always keeping your vaginal area and your bottom covered with underwear or with something else. At no time are you expected to reveal your whole self to a photographer, let alone his camera! I have included elsewhere in this book, details of both model and photographer behaviour, along with their respective expectations at your shoot. It is important that you read this if you are going to model in any of the above genres or any additional ones subsequently in this chapter. The correct protocols and the expected good conduct of both photographer and model is essential in maintaining a just and professional environment!

Art Nude / Nude
Nudity comes in different guises. The art nude is best described with my image here. The model is often posed fully nude but in a variety of 'accepted' classical poses. These type of images may be in full colour or black and white. There is no suggestion of eroticism.
Nude is a wide term, and is itself ambiguous. The model should check with the photographer what kind of nudity is involved. The requirement for the basic nude category should never involve 'open-leg' nudity which is considered as being more 'extreme erotic' or adult nude.

Erotic nude or glamour nude will involve a degree of suggestibility. The

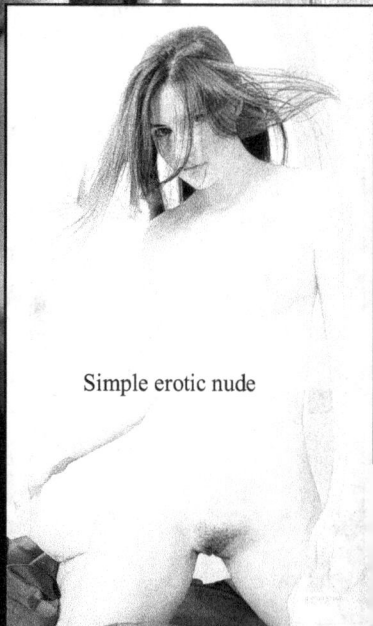

Simple erotic nude

woman is depicted as an object of beauty but also one to be desired either sexually or sensually. It should not involve real pornographic content so there should be nothing in the image associated with masturbation or interaction with other models where sexual touching takes place. It is suggestive—not descriptive!

Fetish

This can involve quite tame modelling, like smoking cigars suggestively, up through into more demanding and more sensitive areas of adult sexual obsessions. If you don't mind being tied up semi-naked with an apple in your mouth, or being depicted as dominated, blood splattered, and often much harder imagery—some bordering on real pornography and some not—then this is for you. And there is money to be made at it too, and a degree of notoriety can be achieved if you are not fazed about doing the more extreme fetish. The thing to do if you want to explore this area, yet you do not wish to get too close to the more 'dark' imagery encompassing the genre of 'Fetish',

Damaged by Mol

is to carefully check out the requirement of each photographer and the shoot itself. Fetish is often toned down to penetrate the world of fashion and provides a sense of danger and a hard-hitting edginess. Often what is taboo in art one day— remember the menstrual-blood-splattered original work of Tracey Emin in 1999—becomes the next massive money-making, lip-gossiping, greatness of tomorrow. But beware!

These genres can be very confusing when a model works with someone like me, a digital artist. What genre best describes my image on the left? The model appears to be peeing milk, possibly from milk injected in her neck from the bottle. Her wet knickers and pubic bulge are sensed. There is danger here with the scissors. She is beautiful, scantily dressed, a woman for certain, but almost a young teenager in her appearance. I created the image as

35

a kind of anti-drug poster where the white-stuff represented a hard-drug. Yet I am also aware of the erotic nature and fetish quality, which are deliberately done by me to charge the image with danger and a sense of taboo! But it would be difficult to pin this sort of work down to explain to a model! I always ask the model if she is comfortable with what I create from the photos and I advise her I will never publish one she feels uncomfortable with. But not all photographers and artists share this degree of honour and fairness with their co-workers. The more you build trust and understanding of an artist/photographer, along with his/her respect for you and your wishes and limits, the better you will get on and the more you can explore as a model.

Adult Nude

Possibly the way to earn money without being a high-end fashion model but with consequences? My 'CENSORED' example below is probably a fairly artistic example of an adult nude pose by the model. In the final image, nothing 'pink' in the Model's vaginal area was visible but the outside of her slightly open vagina was clearly shown. This type of image is often called 'open-leg'. If you hear of the term, 'pink' - for example, "A model does pink", it means she is okay at revealing the soft pink interior of her vagina. It doesn't however in any way indicate or suggest that she is okay with being a PORN STAR!!! Many photographers working in the genres of Adult Nude may be interested in depicting women as beautiful sensual, highly sexual creatures. Many images will be in a Playboy style, suggestive, vaginas on show, but nothing further! A decade or more ago (2 decades?) vaginas being displayed constituted illegal pornography: today, it is

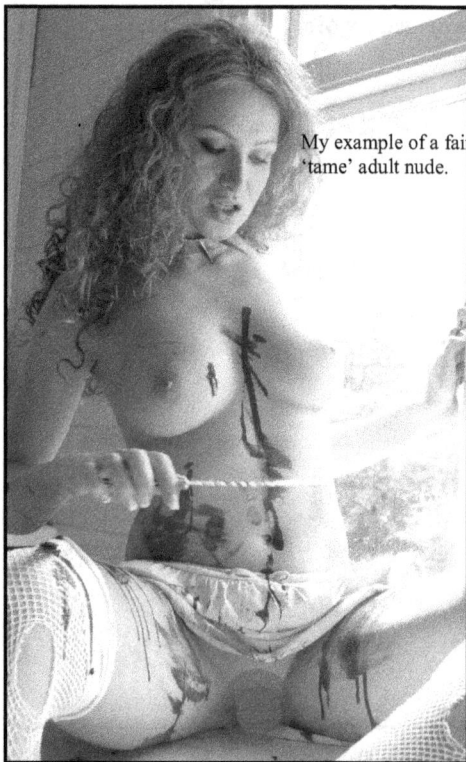

My example of a fairly 'tame' adult nude.

considered another art form! It is important to understand I am not encouraging or discouraging models to consider this genre. The issues are plain to understand. Would your mum like the pictures? Will it affect your career in the future? On the other hand, it can be extremely financially rewarding as the number of models prepared to do this type of work is less than in any of the other genres, and the commercial demand is high for images in this field.

Beyond Adult Nude?!

Although beyond the scope of this book, the next step in female 'modelling' is a form of increased sexuality where sexual interaction with people, toys, and objects are either simulated by the models or is actually carried out! Other forms of Plus Adult Nude may encompass 'wetting' or peeing, just that, on pavements or in view of people. The scale of sexual content increases across the spectrum of all desires and perversions, with each area being considered more extreme, or tamer, according to the mind of each individual on the planet. **None of it is modelling!**

Checking the requirements of the photo-shoot session

It is always best to try and check out the photographer's intention of photograph type if s/he is interested in working with you. Each of the Genre's is only a guide point and only the start of a photographer looking for a model, whilst a model is roughly saying the type of work she is prepared to take on. One thing you can do as a model is to require that all images taken are shown to you after the shoot, and any that you feel are moving you into a realm you are uncomfortable with, you insist on being deleted. You make this part of the deal. I always do! If the photographer refuses at the shoot to fulfil the agreement, you insist all the photographs are deleted and say you are leaving without pay and therefore the contract is off (broken). If s/he refuses, phone the police and explain to them the photographer is holding 'indecent' images of you without your consent. You should make sure to read the entire chapter: The Model Release Form.

I often shoot full frontal nude but I do not expect the model to be comfortable with things she has already clearly stated she does not want to see in an image. Sometimes, during posing and moving, parts are displayed which have *not* been agreed. I always look through the images for this myself to try and protect the model's interests. I delete all I find and show her I am doing that. I delete them on camera and then we look through the images on the computer and repeat the process if we discover any. I earn a lot of trust from the models I work with and on the odd occasion, the model has done a great pose, but this problem exists in the image. She may trust me to keep an image under my promise to post-work it and remove the 'offending' element.

You should only do the same if you really trust the photographer! I do not mean to give the impression that photographers are dishonourable. Most are not. People are good and bad in all realms of life and work. A degree of trust is always involved even when work is under strict contract. The practice of modelling is no different in this respect.

Chapter 3: Getting Your First TF* Shoot

You have your first few photographs uploaded to one or more portfolio sites. You've duly filled in all the information about modelling genres you are interested in doing, your statistics, and now you wait for the zillion or so incoming requests from photographers to work with you paid or Time For Prints/Time for CD. Nothing happens! No incoming messages arrive. No one out there is interested in you. This happens nearly all the time on large successful portfolio sites like 'onemodelplace'. Have you also created a portfolio on other smaller model/photographer portfolio sites like 'Model Mayhem'? It is always a good idea to put a portfolio on several of the web sites. Most of them offer a free start up package. Did you say you were looking to work initially TF* or have you forgotten to mention this? Do your photographs clearly show your face and your full body figure clearly? If you did a write-up about yourself, does it make you sound friendly and easy to work with? For example, did you write something like this.

"Looking to further my modelling career. Need additional prints to extend the range of my portfolio by working TF* with good photographers. Will work up to topless. Pervs and gawkers are not replied to and will be reported to the site admin. Travel costs expected. Photographer must allow a chaperone with me in the studio at all times. Thanks. Lulu."

So, you already think you have a modelling career, do you? And you believe a lot of photographers with portfolios on the web site are not very good at what they do? You imply these things in your opening sentences. You also believe perverts and men only interested in gazing at your naked boobs are the same type of people, and that the portfolio web site you are on is frequented by hordes of both types of men.

Photographers pay out a load of money for cameras, lights, props, computers, printers, paper and ink. They also have to pay rent for studio space, even if it is in their own homes. You expect them to commit their time to you in exchange for you doing the same, yet you also want the luxury of the photographer paying your travel costs when you are going to pay him nothing. Most photographers don't mind if you bring someone along to make sure you are confident and safe, but most of them dislike them being around in the actual space where the shoot takes place. They can distract the model and they also make many photographers nervous by being observed. Almost every photographer I know hates being photographed themselves, so I am quite certain they also do not like to be observed while they are trying to put all their attention into taking the best possible photographs of you. A write-up like this makes you sound like you are an unfriendly, jumped-up, know all! It should come as no surprise to you if you receive no responses at all. It would make me run a mile in the other direction. A better write-up should include a bit about you, a friendly plea or request for photographers to take a chance and risk their time photographing a newbie, and what is in it for them if they do. Photographers wish to spend their time either getting paid for their work, just like you, or creating great images of women for their portfolios to encourage other people to pay them to achieve similar images. Many photographers and artists are not commercial at all. They treat photographing women as an art form, a hobby, or a pleasurable pursuit against a work routine of commercial photography in some other area like wedding portraits, or car accident scenes for insurance companies (to name just two). The following write-up would produce better responses.

"Hi, I'm Lulu. I'm just starting out as a new model. Thought I would try it to see if it's for me. I really need a variety of photo styles to build up my portfolio, so if any of you photographers out there would like to take some pictures of me suitable to build up presence here, please let me know. As I am new, I would love to work TF* with friendly and helpful people until I get to know my way around and before trying to get paid work. Willing to travel but as I only have a part-time job, unless you are quite close, some help with travel costs would be great. I am sincere, friendly, willing to learn, and I love being in front of the camera and receiving direction. Can work up to tasteful topless but would like to receive a few model references, or else bring someone along. They do not need to be in the studio during the shoot. Many thanks for checking me out and for considering me. X"

Doesn't this give a far more approachable and friendlier presentation of yourself? I think so. If yours doesn't read this good, go back to all your web site portfolios and edit them to say something similar but in your own words. What else might you have to offer which may encourage photographers to work with you? Some models have a fantastic wardrobe or unusual clothes. Outfits can be extremely expensive. So if you have a wacky wardrobe set, top line fashion wear, or unique items you make yourself,

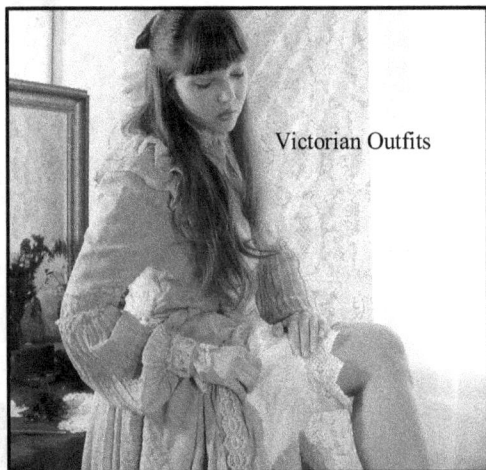

Victorian Outfits

promote these equally as yourself on your portfolio write up. I know some models who have fabulous period clothes of the past. They specialise in retro modelling. I paid the model opposite for a day's shoot as she had an amazing collection of Victorian dresses and undergarments, which allowed me to create a set of cheeky, saucy, Victorian type titillating prints in 3D.

40

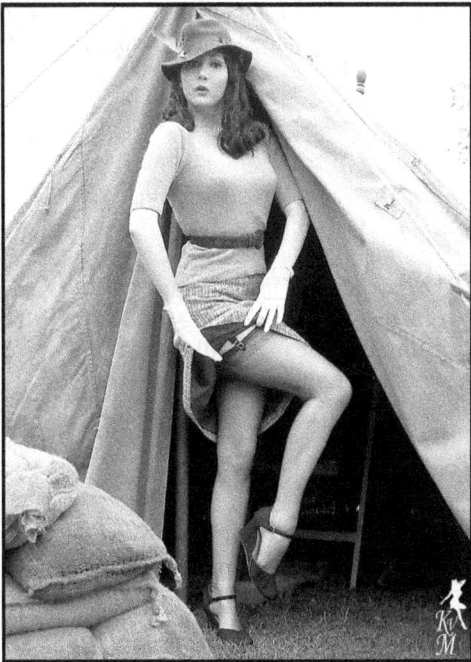

A good example of modelling in a niche genre and using clothes and study to emulate images from a bygone age.

Are other niche areas emerging? Do you look a little bit like a famous person?

Kitten von Mew—Britain's No.1 Vintage Pin-Up, specialising in 1930's, 40's and 50's Burlesque Artist performing in London, Sheffield and Milan—has made an art form of modelling vintage shots. These are some of her images.

You have your portfolios in place with the right attitude reflected in your remarks and the 'details' area about yourself, and wham... responses start to come in. Now what? The most likely thing is that you are offering some degree of sensuality: lingerie, implied nude, topless, see-thru, or higher levels of exposure. The world is the world it is. You can't change it and 1 vote every 4 or 5 years hasn't changed it much in the past. If you are not prepared to enter any of these categories, even to model for very tasteful and graceful exposure, you are going to need to work a great deal harder to find paid work through a model portfolio site unless you look like a million dollars in every single respect. Few people do, and amateur, pro, and the commercial industry know that too!

For the moment I will deal with the issue of receiving responses for those prepared for a degree of body-exposure and then we will look at the possible and probable shortage of responses for models not prepared for more risqué, yet tasteful, forms of modelling. You are likely to get a mix of offers for TF* and some paid work. If you only get offers of TF* work for now, you still need to take them once you have sifted, to ensure you build up your portfolio. You should see the whole thing as a marketing exercise: you have to be wanted for a photo shoot more than someone else on the site. You need imaginative, safe, respectful, highly accomplished photographers and artists to want to work with you. The better they are, the more likely the images produced will excel and promote you towards paid work. I recently did a TF* with a lovely girl and her max level was topless and implied nude. By looking at her and realising her structure, assets, and defects, I was able to create some great images of her straight from camera. We put six images on one portfolio site and within 1 hour, she had 9 responses, with 3 of them offering her paid work within the limits of her degree of exposure.

I have put some of the images, reduced in size, on the following two pages to give you some ideas of what images you need to get in your portfolio and why. I recommend you look carefully at these and my notes. The images are massively reduced in size and presented here in b&w but you'll get the point.

The type of replies you are likely to get will vary from the genuine photographer, the amateur, the semi-professional, and the downright exploiter. Fortunately, from experience, most replies are genuine and in good faith. The world is not populated with a majority of sex maniacs, Hannibal Lectors, and pornographers, despite what news items and feeds you listen to. The majority of human-beings range from good to boring, with a tiny majority being bad. Alas, the business of selling news would have us all believe differently because 'human fear' sells news. So ninety-nine percent of photographers on portfolio sites are not bad people. Some might be bad photographers, have different image genre interests to those you wish to model for, but most of them are decent enough for you to consider their responses seriously. Some may wish to pay. Many will wish to work on a trade basis. Nearly all of them will not be trying to cause you any direct harm. But you will need to sieve through the replies and work out which ones are going to be best for you. I will help you with this after you have looked at the pictures.

This is the model's main image. The one seen when anyone first hits her portfolio on a site! She has decided she is comfortable working up to topless and implied nude. When a new portfolio is created on a model portfolio site, it is common for the site to display the portfolio's main image on a special area where photographers can see who is new.

This is a major opportunity that only comes once. Most photographers watch this area, hoping to shoot the next best female who arrives. It is competitive both from a model's point of view and the photographers—themselves having limited time, resources, and image aims, just like you! It is critical to get attention at this moment and kick-start yourself into a world where other women are competing to build their portfolio better than yours. Other models can be your friends too, but first we must engage in a game of winning our aims.

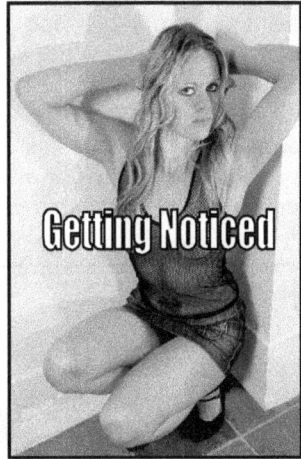

Getting Noticed

This is one of the model's main images, one of several that a photographer will see when arriving at her portfolio. It says a lot: she is pretty, knows good taste from bad taste (the hand hiding her peek-thru topless body) and she is not staring at the camera, or you in a challenging way, which means a photographer can take time to look at her and consider her. The light is intriguing: not flash photography, but taken by a simple warm light. Does this add something to the desire to work with this model, to see her this way almost like a classic and desirable woman from a bygone age? Yes. It does. Most photographers are men. Much of their desire to photograph women is also mixed with, but safely separated from, their innate desire to encounter new women. Photography of women relies upon this aspect of a male photographer's psyche. How else should he know how a woman will appeal or not to the masses. This is not the opening image. The first one showed quickly the degree of work range limitation. But here the model reinforces her wish to model in an area no higher than topless and implied nude. So she makes certain to show herself in toned-down form of sexuality called 'sensuality' to ensure her main image does not convey erotic-modelling intent. (continued on page 46)

Broadening your appeal!

Becky T
by Mar Jan 2009

These are the remaining three photos our model selected for her free portfolio. Image [1] is a nice slightly, deliberately, blurred shot to show her very naturally: 'girl next door' look. Image [2] slightly revealing, showing her with a more serious expression. Image [3] is softly 'sexy' without being overtly sexual. A single 300 watt tungsten light, like the floodlight's people put up at the rear of their houses, was used. Flash lights do not produce very atmospheric pictures.

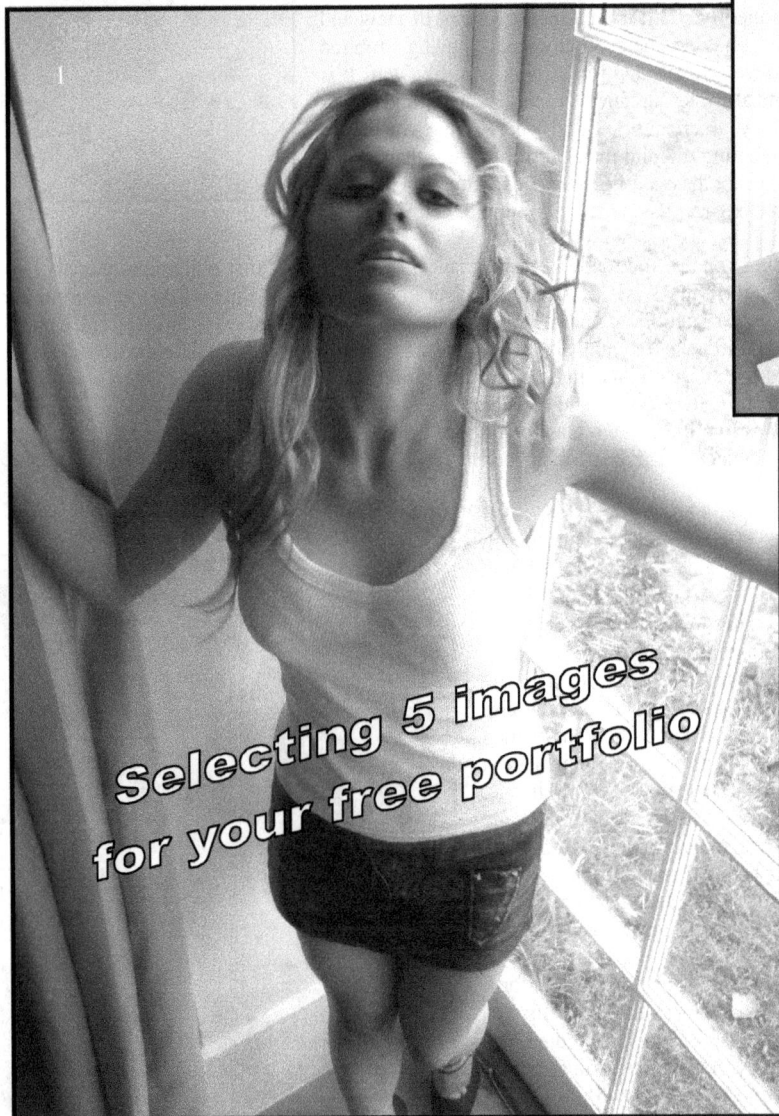

Selecting 5 images for your free portfolio

3

Great Lips. Atmospheric Shadows on the model's face.

Loose, peek-beneath top, but tasteful, with nipples covered.

Stocking tops revealed, adds a sensual element.

(continued from Page 43) The first thing to do when you receive a response from a photographer is to go and check his/her portfolio. What are the photos or art images like? Do they impress you? How attractive are the other models he has used? What genres do his photos fit into? Are they in the areas you wish to model in? Have models left references on his page? He is an amateur, a semi-pro, or a pro? Is he offering paid work or TF*? Does he have his/her own studio? How far away? Is the photographer offering to visit you at your home and photograph (*shoot*) you?

If any of the following are true, take my advice below.

Photographer wants to shoot me at my home.

No! No! No! Never, ever, allow a photographer to know where you live until such time that you have worked with him and feel is he honourable and trustworthy. Reply to him and tell him, "Thanks", but you have now got some TF* shoots arranged.

The photographer is located a long way from you?

Train fares and petrol cost money and time. The further away, the greater the cost. If the photographer produces amazing photos or art, it many be worth it. Ask if s/he will pay your travel costs or share them.

Most of the photos in the portfolio are glamour nude or erotica with a lot of suggestive nudity.

Unless you specifically wish to do that type of modelling, reply to say, "Thanks," but you are looking for less exposed images of yourself for your portfolio.

The photos are quite mixed: some clothed, some topless, a few nude, but they are impressive.

If he is not too far from you, reply and ask if he will shoot you within your genre. Tell him what that is. If he replies yes, ask him to supply email addresses of recent models so you can obtain references about him. Will he allow a chaperone?

Amateur, pro, or semi-pro is not really important to you if their images are good. Many photographers don't have a standard studio but work in a space at their home. This is quite acceptable. Do not work with any photographer unable to provide you with at least three models email addresses and who won't allow you to take a companion with you. Always do this the first time you work with a new photographer. If they supply models emails, write to them, and check out their experience and what they think about the photographer. If you get no replies, write to the photographer and ask for more references. If you don't get all good replies, don't go!

If a photographer is asking to pay you, consider what type of work the money is for. Is it the type of work you have said you will do in your portfolio, or work he wants to do, even if it's not in your portfolio: erotic, art nude, topless, implied nude? Reply to him and ask. If you are up for the paid job, ask if he will let you have copies of photos on CD to use in your portfolio. He will want to know your rates. If you are a 'newbie' keep your prices low to ensure you get the work and pick up experience. You can increase your rates later once you have done a few jobs and gained some experience. What do you charge if paid work is offered? Everyone has their own price according to the degree of exposure. By this, I mean: how clothed or not clothed? How erotic, if the work involves nudity or part clothed?

At the time of writing, I regard the following rates as an average charged by experienced models. I have paid as little as £10.00 an hour for full frontal art nude and erotic nude and I have paid £50.00 an hour for the same with more expensive models.

RATES PER HOUR

Clothed:	£10 .00 - £15.00
Lingerie & See-thru:	£15 .00 - £20.00
Topless	£20 .00 - £25.00
Implied Nude:	£20 .00 - £30.00
Art Nude:	£20 .00 - £40.00
Adult Nude/Pink/Erotic Nude:	£20 .00 - £50.00

To get started, try and work to the minimum rate plus travel costs. Most models stipulate a minimum rate of 2 hours and apply discounts for 4 hours (half-day) rate and a full day. So instead of a maximum charge of 8 hours at, say - £40.00 per hour, a model would probably charge £250.00 for the day.

Fetish can range from simply smoking, clothed, to bondage and more extreme forms of imagery. Most fetish models will apply a rate based roughly on the degree of acceptability to them for the required work. The rate for extreme Fetish modelling, not of a type falling into the bounds of pornography or adult performer, can be as low as £15.00 and hour and as high as £60.00 an hour.

A Model starting out may often do part TF* and part paid. This enables her to have a right to a CD of prints for free use only on her portfolios. Obviously, she would cut her rates for this. Remember, all rates are negotiable and you can always try reducing them if the photographer says he can't afford you. It is easy to reply back with reduced rates but you can't reply back and ask for more.

Actively Seeking Work
Putting up a free five image portfolio onto several portfolio web sites is just a start at trying to get both TF* and paid work. Many experienced models actively seek photographers to work with either to broaden or refresh their portfolios by doing TF* work, or simply to find photographers that their own look and type of modelling will appeal to. If you only have a free portfolio,

you will probably not be able to carry out advanced searches on the portfolio site but you may be able to search through the forums. A small fee to the Portfolio web site will increase the number of images you can load and also help you search for appropriate TF* photographers and paid work. Almost any female model of a fair shape and good with good looks can easily receive many enquiries from male photographers offering to work TF* if she is prepared to work topless and beyond.

No Responses

If you receive no enquiries from photographers interested in working with you, don't get disheartened. The probable reason will be because you have offered to work in a narrow and non-exposure related set of genres. The way to increase your potential for work is to offer more: a good wardrobe, a make-up artist (a friend?), some lingerie work if it is fairly tame and not-erotic. Other ways is to approach photographers who are not interested in topless or nude work. Many of these may be Pros who wish to build up commercial portfolios for their potential commercial clients. You may have to work a bit harder but you will still find work if you are patient and focused.

Some Do's and Don'ts

Do Maintain Privacy For Your Safety

Do not give away your real email address to photographers you don't know, even if you are exchanging messages regarding a first shoot with them. Use the web-portfolio site system, which keeps your real name, your real email address, and your postal address private.

Don't Waste Money On Rip-Offs

Do not pay to have your first portfolio made. Some agencies (many) offer test shoots to see if you are acceptable, and then inform you they will sign you up, but you will need a portfolio. I have met models who have paid £750 for 5 bad photos which I could have done in my sleep in a few hours for less than £100. Why pay anyway? If someone can get you work because they think you have the right stuff, let them spend money on you, not the other way round. The idea of women needing modelling portfolios has led to the business of agencies which are in reality non-agencies, ripping off the young, the new, and the inexperienced—the same as in many other areas of work and our society. Me? I would hang them for exploiting innocence!

Don't Sign Anything

Sign nothing unless you really know what you are signing. There are forms associated with modelling for pay, and different forms for TF* work. They detail both your and the photographer's rights of ownership, copyright, and terms of use of any photographs taken of you by him/her. Read my chapter on Model Release and TFP forms! Do not sign an agency contract on the day it might be offered to you. Take it away and seek advice.

Don't Visit New Photographers...

...**alone**, or unless you have made proper checks with models who have worked with them (recently, if possible). Always do this and you will remain safe and be comfortable at the photo-shoot.

Don't Hang Around...

...if you feel uncomfortable for any reason at a photo shoot. Your instincts may make you think something doesn't feel right. A photographer should offer to leave the studio or photo-session space, or provide you with a private space, to change clothes and outfits. If you are about to do nude work, this may not happen as s/he will assume you are okay with this. If you are not doing nude work, it should not be expected for you to remove clothes and put on new ones in the photographer's presence. Ask for privacy. If the photographer even begins to discuss it instead of immediately understanding, just leave! Don't talk about it. Just say you are going. If s/he then offers you a private space to change, still leave!

In time, you will get to know the good guys from the iffy ones. Until then, follow my advice. A photographer should respect you and care about how you feel and think. You are not a clothes horse nor a 'dog's body'. You should not behave like a diva either. You should look for the same respect and courtesy in your work that you would expect in any other true profession. And you should behave the same.

Don't Let People Down

If you make arrangements with photographers, keep them. Be on time. If you can't make a shoot due to illness or a change in circumstances, ensure you contact the photographer in good time or your name will soon get around as that of someone unreliable!

Don't Use Your Real Name

Create a modelling name for yourself. We call it a model alias. This will ensure no-one will learn your real name unless you want them to. Most models will tell a photographer their real name once they have worked with them and trust them. But you do not have to unless you are signing an agreement like a contract or a model release form. Pick a name to sum you up, either your area of modelling or how you look. Red-haired? How about these: Viking-queen, Banshee, Autumn-Annie, Scarlet-Witch, Burning-Amber.... I am sure you get my point!

Chapter 4: Going To Your First Shoot

Getting there

You've got your first shoot lined up. It might be a TF* to help you get more pictures for your portfolio of it might be a paid job. Either way, you should treat both types as though they were a paid shoot. By that, I mean you should be professional, on time, and ready. Make sure to shower or wash properly before you go. Give yourself plenty of time. Go to bed at a reasonable hour the night before so you are fresh, alert, and not panicking in the morning.

You should have done everything mentioned in the previous chapter about checking out the photographer: model reference checks or have arranged to take a chaperone with you. Do your make-up and hair the way you normally would if you were going out for a night on the town or clubbing. Wear clothes that show you off right from the start when you arrive: short skirts or figure-hugging dresses, neat tops. Make sure you have clean, crisp, fresh lingerie under your top clothes, clean knickers and bra. Wear the newest underwear you can so you feel confident. Do not use hair lacquer on your hair. Any other hair holding gel or light lotion to dampen down any split-ends or fuzziness is okay, but if you hard-spray longish hair and the photographer wants to blow it around with a fan, it isn't going to budge!

Are you taking outfits with you? Pack them neatly in a small suitcase with wheels. Don't forget a few extra things: hairbrush, clothes, ornaments like dress jewellery and necklaces, wrist bands, ear-rings, shoes, tights, stockings, hold-ups, spare make-up and hairgrips, bobbles etc., Going by train? Got the tickets or web print out of your connections and times? Going by car—take the address with you and if you don't have sat-nav, a map! Ensure you have the photographers mobile number on your mobile, which should have been fully charged that evening. Leave in good time so any connection or road delays won't cause you to be late. If you arrive early, simply find somewhere local to go and have a cup of tea so you kill some time in order to arrive punctually. Arriving too early is almost as bad as too late, because the photographer may not be ready for you. If you find your train cancelled or you get stuck in a traffic jam, please be certain to phone the photographer and let him/her know.

Always try and ring the photographer the day before your model-shoot session just so that he knows you are still coming and to make sure he hasn't forgotten either! Some photographers are so busy, they would forget their names without being reminded!

The Photo-Shoot

Okay. You got there. This is it then. You may be nervous but try to be calm and relaxed. Remember, this is not an audition for a starring role in the next box-office smash, it's just someone taking photographs. No big deal! First thing then is to covertly check your safety, especially if you didn't take a chaperone. What is the place like? Is it a studio or some space in his/her house. Many photographers use their home, remember, as studio space is expensive. Has the photographer got some of his/her images hanging up? Let's assume the photographer is a he. Did he greet you in a polite and caring way? Is he friendly? Does he ask about your journey, and if you had any problems finding the place? When you enter the photo-session space, has he got lights, stands and tripods set-up? Does it look like he is in the business or (passion of) photography? If you are confronted with a guy, a camera, a bedroom, no lights other than a simple tiny flash light on a small digital camera, this may be your first unlucky choice. He may not be a valid photographer destined to leave behind a legacy of great photos and images, but just an ordinary guy who likes taking fairly candid picture of pretty girls.

This is unlikely if you did the proper checks, but hey—we all make mistakes, what do you do now though if it's true? Well, you could leave. You could stay if you feel safe in his presence and earn some money. Just be careful to stay within your degree of exposure and genre limits: *don't take more clothes off than what you planned to before you started out! If the guy starts being suggestive, or makes overt sexual comments to you, or touches you in places he should not be doing—leave!*

Let's assume, like in 99.5% of cases, everything is okay and he is a real photographer. What should happen next? He may, as I always do, sit down with you for a chat over a cup of tea or soft drink. The idea here is to relax you and for him to get to know more about you. He wants to know what will work best for you. Do not be discouraged or uneasy if he looks at you a bit too long. If he is good, he is also making mental notes about your shape, your face, and what camera angles will best flatter you. He may ask what you brought along and want to see the clothes and stuff. That's good as he is showing proper concern and interest for you. You should be polite too. Be on your best behaviour. Don't swear. Some people are greatly offended and put off by unnecessary foul language. Be friendly, smile, show interest in his work. Being friendly doesn't not mean throwing passes at him. I am sure you know that but I am just making sure.

He may suggest what to wear or ask you to pick something. He might have a whole set of ideas he wants to try out, especially if he is more of an artist than a straight photographer. If you have not agreed to any kind of nudity or partial exposure, he may still explore that with you, either now in conversation, or later, during the shoot. This is not a bad thing. He is making sure he understands clearly the reasons why you are limiting your capacity in modelling, and as long as he is not constantly trying to persuade you to go full nude, you should not find this an unanticipated thing. Most photographers love taking photographs of women with less clothes on. It doesn't mean to say you are going to, or that he actually wants you to go further against your wishes. Some models would love to work nude as there is far more paid work for them, but they are shy, or lack confidence, so the photographer may be seeing if these are your reasons. I often do that because it helps me understand more about my freedom to photograph a clothed model in possibly more risqué shots. Be honest with him. If this is your first shoot, let him know that. If you are a bit nervous, tell him. If the photographer is a skilled and sensitive human-being, he will take all your concerns and newness into account, and you will have met a good one. If he shows no such tendencies, bad luck, carry on and make a mental note not to offer him the chance to shoot you again in the future. You may be the next best thing to modelling just waiting to happen once you have picked up some experience, and you are going to remember the good guys from the not so good later.

Make sure he offers you a private secluded place or room to change your clothes. I always leave the area and tell the model to shout when she's ready. The exceptions are sometimes when the model and I have worked well together before, and she trusts me more just to look away until she says she's ready—or the model is going to pose nude and she doesn't mind about me being present while she undresses.

You change into your first outfit, assuming it is a clothed shoot, and you have checked your make-up and hair. Try not to fuss too long with these things, especially if the photographer is paying you an hourly rate. You take up position in front of the lights and camera and you are ready to go. Now what? Many glamour models have learnt a set of poses and can run them off—one after the other. Many models in other genres have an idea of how they look to appear alluring or interesting. You are new. You will probably have no such learnt expertise. Ask the photographer how he wants you to pose. A good photographer will direct and guide you on posing and expressions. The shoot might be a bit slow to start with as the photographer tries out various angles and lighting to see what works best for your look. Give him and yourself time to get acquainted through the medium of the camera. He should offer you sound bites: "Left a little. Look here over my shoulder, Drop your chin a little. No. Too much. Lift a little. Yes. Spot on. Hold it. {FLASH} Well done. Keep it. {FLASH}. Ok. Great." etc. He is the director and the expectation is on him to direct you, not the other way round. If he is useless, you are not going to hear any of that, so you are going to have to help the idiot! It's like sitting next to a driver who knows how to manage the car safely but doesn't know where to drive. You are going to have to come up with the ideas, the poses, and basically do everything but take the pictures. Unlucky. It happens with some photographers.

I want you to realise this is completely different to you having ideas and working with a good photographer. A good one constantly has new ideas or a whole mental tool box of previous ideas he can repeat with you, and he will love to hear and share your ideas too. After all, you two have got together to make some great images, paid or not. Just in case you have got stuck with a dummy photographer, here is Mol's emergency bail-out short posing course for new models. Most of these can be used as standard poses in any genre. Where they are more risqué, I have annotated them so you will know. Take a look at the notes and images on the next few pages to understand a bit more about making the best of your body, posture, and your face. If nothing else, it will get you to start trying these in the mirror at home.

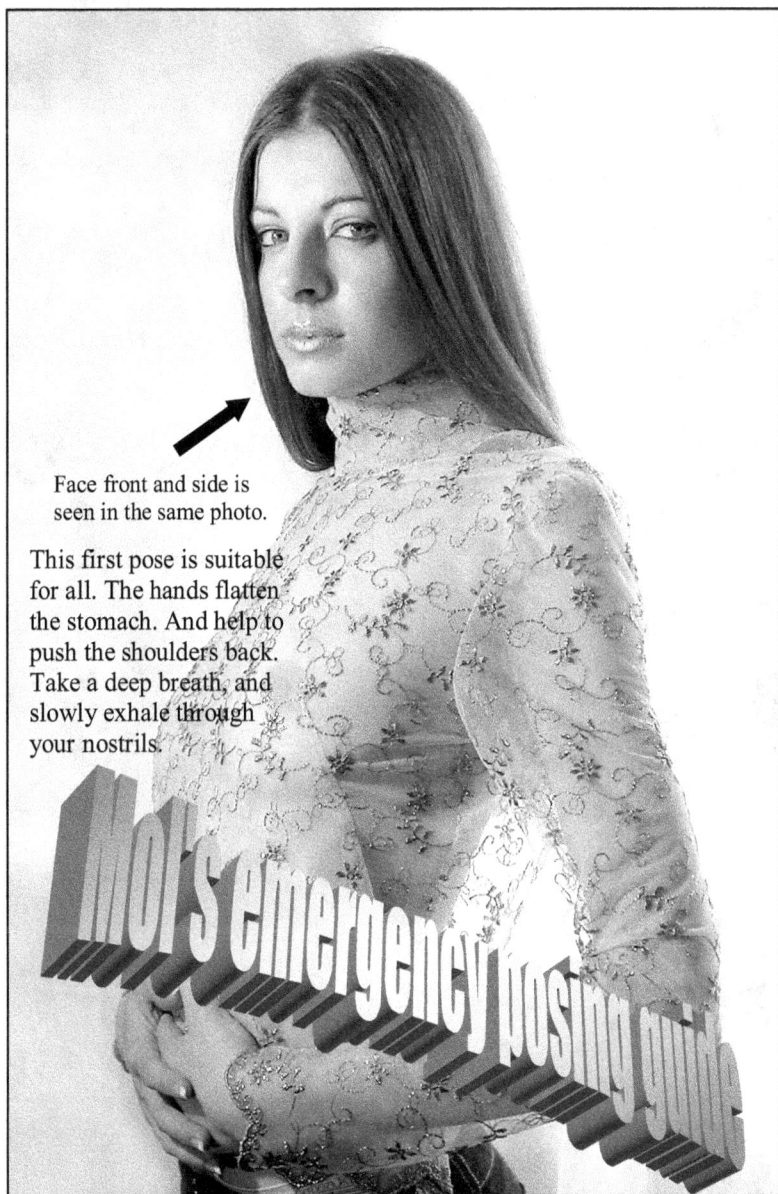

Face front and side is seen in the same photo.

This first pose is suitable for all. The hands flatten the stomach. And help to push the shoulders back. Take a deep breath, and slowly exhale through your nostrils.

This increases breast firmness and helps you bring your waist in. You can use it to create a great shape (curve) for your back.

Sitting & kneeling allows the photo to be filled more fully than standing poses. The model here makes body shapes to create gentle interesting content.

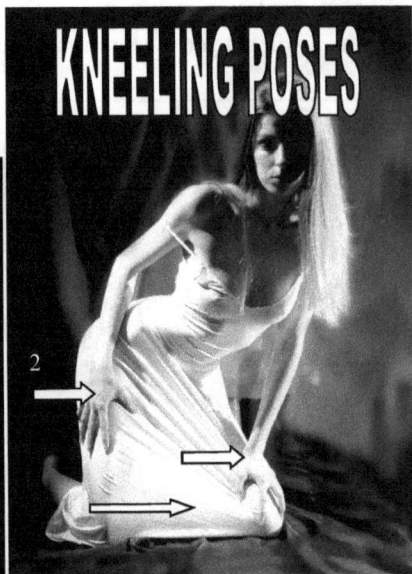

KNEELING POSES

{1} Model turns at waist.

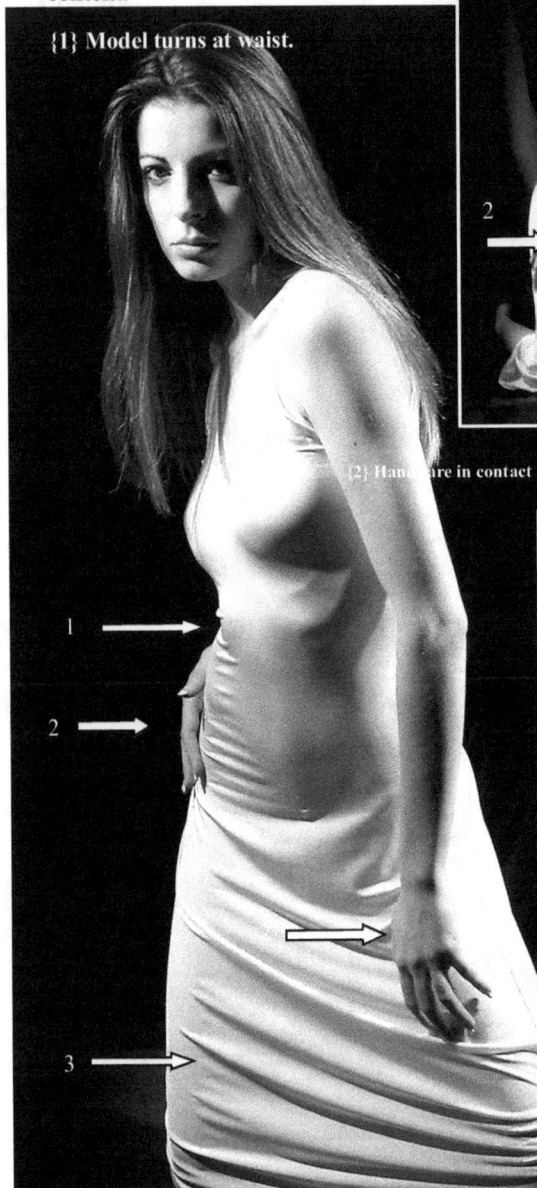

{2} Hands are in contact with body, not dangling.

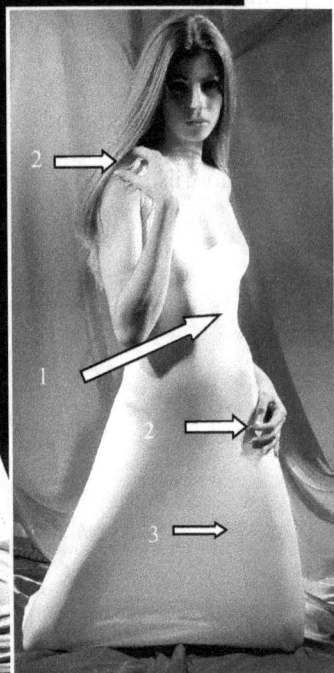

{3} Legs astride to build up shape and make waist look narrow.

ACTING POSES

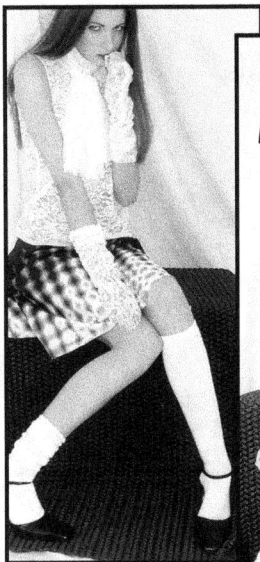

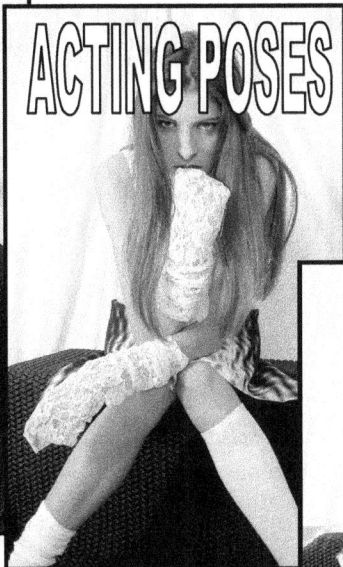

Here is Beth's schoolgirl look: legs awkward, hunched (shy) shoulders. Nervousness is depicted in 1 and 2 with glove-chewing. Tear your hair out in frustration {3}.

FASHION POSES

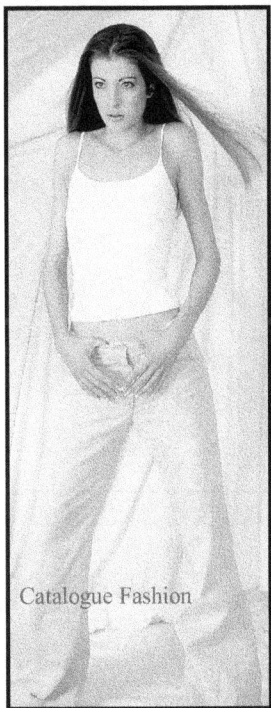

Catalogue Fashion

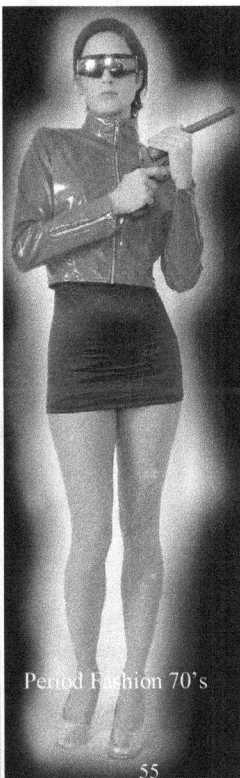

Period Fashion 70's

Contemporary

Notice that shape and posture is important. See how each model is communicating a message with her stance. You can look through magazines and practice the poses in them.

55

Glamour today ranges from traditional, almost Pin-Up posing to far less calm and a lot more risqué imagery. Here are some of the more traditional type of images. Do you see the way the model is posing in a girly, gently suggestive way without being provocative. On the opposite page, you can study a few poses for the increased sexuality of the styles more prevalent in the last decade. Remember… you are acting. Practice in front of a mirror!

GLAMOUR POSES

Screaming, shouting,
open mouth, suggests
dynamic emotional
reaction... like orgasm!

Facial expression with
eyes wide suggests the
same.

That should give you a few starting ideas. I have covered more on Posing in a later chapter, so right now—let's get on with your first shoot. Some photographers and/or models like music playing at the photo-session. Me? I can't stand it. You do what the photographer prefers as regards of music because some will welcome it and some won't. Most photographers work using flash lights. Maybe you have never seen professional flash lighting? They are bright! So don't get caught gazing right into them when the flash fires or else you won't be seeing much else for the next minute or so. If the photographer wants you to try altering your pose slightly for each successive shot in a series, do not shift your pose unless the flash fires. It takes a few seconds for the flash to charge up enough power to fire again after a shot is taken, and you may well hear a click or beep from the photographer's camera, and think you can take up the next pose, but unless the flash fires... don't.

Also remember, the photographer is thinking about all the technical stuff too, and you, and the bits of you which are working for you, clothes, expressions, movement, hair, blinking, mouth expressions, your breathing, posture, and much more, but at a certain point he has to press the button and capture the best compromise of tens of variables. He will capture just 1/125th of a possible 3 to 5 seconds of reposing. This is 1 tiny moment of 750 possible moments in 5 seconds. Since his trigger finger can only operate at 1/10 of a second to what he sees, he is going to miss the exact thing most of the time, unless you learn to move and stay, move and stay, move and stay: like a beat! He will do the same. Shoot and wait. Shoot and wait. Well, at least in that kind of session activity. There are various lighting sets the photographer may use, from studio flash lighting, static tungsten lights, daylight, ultra-violet, stage lighting, experimental lighting, or a mix of all of these, and you are the subject which has to be lit. The attention he takes to lighting will give you clues about how good he is. Most photographers set up a few expensive flash lights which freeze your motion, wipe the shadows behind you, and illuminate you so all depth of you, including imperfections in your face and skin are wiped by flat light. Great—you say! Yes, this is the bog-standard way of doing time-honoured fashion and glamour photography. It works and it's great. Some photographers will do some of that and then move on. They are the ones to watch and learn from because they are trying to capture you in various styles and guises. These are the best photographers who reach out across all genres and technologies to master their field. Learn from them and you will soon be the model in demand. It is not just looks, shape, or form, it is about working with people who are uncommonly apt in their work. As a model, you can't just model, you have to find synergy with the other members of the team. Sometimes, most times, the Team is you and one other—the photographer. Other times it may be many: hair stylist, make-up artist, fashion stylist, lighting assistant etc. Non-high fashion models, working to procure work via internet sites and online portfolio presentation, will most often work with a photographer and no additional people. As a model, you are one-half of the creative process!

Chapter 5: Midway & End - Your First Shoot

Midway

You've been working for about an hour or so. How is it going? Is the photographer directing you properly? Is he showing you sets of images on the camera as you proceed so you can check your expressions and poses to see if you can improve on what is on the camera so far? If not, suggest it. If he says no, tell him that by looking, you can see how to help him get the looks and expressions he wants. Only an idiot would refuse you. Don't ask after every photo. An hour in is a good time. Maybe you are working outside and it's winter. Are you cold? If the photographer doesn't think of it (he will have all *his* clothes on), ask him if you can warm yourself up. Where? Car, café, by putting a lot of clothes on. If you get very cold working in winter by wearing less clothes than you wear normally, often standing around instead of moving, you can get very ill. You won't be doing much work for the next 3 months if you catch pneumonia. It is up to you to protect your health if s/he is so involved in the shoot, he forgets to consider your safety and comfort.

Modelling and photography consumes enormous amounts of nervous energy. There is pressure on both sides to get the right shots in a limited period of time. If you have arranged to work say, 4 hours, you should take a break for a cup of tea half way through. It's a good time to review the photos taken so far, and you can tell the photographer that the time out is not part of the fee-paying time. If you are on a TF*, then insist on the break anyway! Also, if you have both agreed for you to have a CD of the shoot, or that you are to check through the photos and okay them (common where nudity or partial nudity is involved), leave time for that. Check your watch subtly and make sure you do check the images and have a CD burnt. A minimum of 30 minutes after you have dressed and collected all your stuff together is required.

It's the end of the shoot. You have hopefully checked through the images on the photographers PC (not just his camera), ensured deletion of any showing too much of you if you have restricted your 'in-print' degree of nudity exposure, and you are almost finished. If it's a paid shoot, ensure now you are paid what you agreed. If it's a TF* shoot, ask that if s/he manipulates or changes the images significantly, not just post-works them to tidy up lighting and remove blemishes, then you will wish to see them before agreeing they can be used. The reason for this is difficult for a lot of people to appreciate. I will explain it in one easy paragraph: using computer and editing software, it is possible to remove your clothes, paint in pubic hairs, and worse, or simply take your face and stick it on a photo of another person doing something sexually extreme. Most photographers are actually honourable. Also, they do not really have the time or skill with image editors to do what I have just explained, but some can. One or two may be less than honourable. Always make any TF* agreement include this one stipulation. I know of a very young girl (13) who went with her mum to a shoot where everything was okay. Several months later, the police knocked on her door because they had found the photographer selling porn images of women with the young girl's head transferred onto one of the 'performing' women'. It is a rare thing, and you should not be paranoid about this, but why not protect yourself from images being published on the net or in print in which they are not what you posed for completely as they have been altered. Let me show you what I mean.

I work with a model called Eve. That is her model alias name. Eve is great as an artist's model. She is okay with Art Nude work but many of my images extend beyond the simple meaning of 'art nude'. Eve and I decided to do a modern Vampire-inspired image. If you look over on the page opposite you will see the photo she modelled for, which I took. She is wearing a thong. Eve was not bothered about removing the thong but neither of us were certain about what might work best in the final image. An image, mind you, that she knew I will build afterwards using this shot. I decide when working on this image that it worked better without the thong. I am quite skilled at image manipulation: the act of taking a photograph as a digital image and then changing it manually using image editing tools on my computer. I was not too concerned about doing this because I more or less know what Eve would feel 'comfortable' with. She has a passion like me for movie-inspired dramatic imagery. So I removed the thong digitally and altered the image by quite a lot to achieve the effect I saw in my head. The final image is larger than what you are about to see and has many changes which are quite extreme in the areas of sexuality and horror. I have only published a detail from it here to demonstrate my point. Turn the next page to see a detail of how it looked after I altered it, and then please come back here straight after.

Spot the difference?

Supposing the photographer you are working with at your first shoot has the same skill as me, and you only wish to limit yourself to topless or bikini, or have nothing exposed at all. How do you ensure, paid or not, what will become of the photo he takes? This is as yet an unsolved problem within UK law. Technology has moved at such a fast rate that many areas of image legality and rights have failed to keep pace. You can use 'trust' and/or

Actual Untouched
Photo of Eve!

After I Retouched
the photo of Eve!

62

minimise the problem by using a Model Release or TF* form. Many exist. All are different. I have created a few which might prove useful to you later in this book. For now though—just be aware of the possibilities when you pop off to your first paid or TF* shoot. Incidentally... I agree all post-worked images with the models who posed for the original photo, to ensure they are comfortable with my final work. We are all different. We have various boundaries and perceptions. I like to put people first. Some people don't share this, therefore please don't think everyone out there shares an artist's honourable aims and considerations. A lot don't!

Now, where were we? Ah. Yes—the end of the shoot. Make sure to look for everything you brought with you and put it all in your bag. Left items are expensive and time-consuming to return: clothes, make-up, props, clips, brushes, shoes, mobile phone, handbag, purse, jewellery, piercings, watch, CD, copy of signed Model Release Form or TF* form etc. Likewise, check you are not also packing the photographers borrowed props, phone, or clothes in with yours. Got your map? Know your directions if you are driving, or your train time back? Say goodbye to the photographer. If it feels right—a double peck, one either side of the cheek, otherwise a handshake, and off you go.

If you are returning early evening by train, tube, or bus, most of the time spent on our transport system is relatively safe despite the terrible headlines you see every week in the dailies. There might be a little bit of concern when you leave the station the other end and its an hour or more later, dark, winter, and you are going to be walking alone in empty streets. You are tired. You wore great make-up and girly clothes to the shoot, but this may not be the best way to look walking down empty dark roads at night. Three choices exist: you arrange for a friend, partner, or boyfriend to meet you at the distant station, you take a cab home for the last leg of the journey, or you plan for this in advance and put on a great big cover-yourself shapeless coat before you get off the train. It doesn't hurt to slip into the shapeless mass of the ordinary and not stand out sometimes! When you get home, you are going to be tired, yet still feel excited by the day. You will want to run to the computer and load that CD and really go searching through those photos. Have something to eat and drink first then take a look, but make sure not to go to bed too late. The CD will still be there tomorrow. Good sleep and rest is as important as working out and keeping trim. If this was your first TF* or paid shoot, it might be a good idea to write some notes down on what you learnt and what you can do next time to improve your modelling or some other aspect of your experience. Do it. Make a folder or a file box and store your TF* form or model release in it so that they build up before you lose the details of the day. This way, you have something on record later on to refer to.

To end this chapter, just in case no-one else tells you, I want to say: well done! You have gone out and done something which 95 percent of women will never do. Even if you decide modelling is not for you, hopefully you will have had a great, interesting day—safely executed, remembered, and retold in the future. Maybe... just maybe... you will have caught the bug too, and you will want to do it again and again?

Chapter 6: Forms and Legal Stuff

UK Copyright Laws

In the USA, Europe, and the UK, the photographer has natural legal copyright to any and all photographs s/he takes. Privacy laws do not prevent a photographer from photographing you in the street or publishing those photographs. Both of these legal positions are important to understand. As a model, when you work with a photographer either paid for modelling or unpaid, the photographer has all the rights to the photographs and you have none. If the photographer says to you that he is okay about you using the photos for your online portfolio and you have nothing from him in writing proving his consent, then you have no formal legal right to publish them on the net or anywhere else.

Time For Prints Form

When working TF*, you should ensure that both you and the photographer sign an agreement stating in simple and precise terms what each of your rights are. You should agree, before the TF* shoot, what form you both intend to sign. It must be the same form, and both of your signatures are needed to make that document valid. We will call this form a "Time For Prints" form (or agreement). If you fail to obtain a copy of this signed form for your records, the photographer can insist you cease using the photos of you, and you will have no written proof that he had originally agreed that you can use them. Be warned that your time modelling free could work against you if you work with unscrupulous photographers.

Model Release Form

A magazine or other publication interested in publishing a photographer's work, will almost certainly ask him or her for a copy of the Model Release Form before they will publish. The form is a signed agreement from a model who has normally been paid by the photographer. Models working TF* may also sign a model release form, or this aspect can be contained in a section of the TF* form itself. The release form is a formal method to say the model grants the photographer all rights to the photographs s/he has taken of her during the photo session. The form may carry additional stipulations or caveats to advantage either parties or to protect them. For example, the model may not wish her real name to be associated with the images, and instead— insists only her model alias is ever used. I should restate here that the photographer owns the photographs he has taken whether you sign a release form or not, but most professional publications will insist on seeing the form to avoid any possible future legal implications concerning copyright.

The Model Release Form and the TF* form both traditionally advantage the photographer over the model. The standard TF* form is normally the worse of the two, and because of this, I have endeavoured to promote a Fair

Trade TF* and Model Release Form to ensure the model's rights are protected as equally as the photographer's. This has expectedly met with much disapproval from many photographers who are used to superior control instead of fairness. I would strongly urge you to download these forms from my internet web site and use them, especially when working TF*. Most fair photographers will not disagree to using them. I have printed a version of the form here along with descriptive notes so you can understand each point. An outline regarding the legal aspect of Model Release Forms is available on the Internet from Wikipedia at this address:

http://en.wikipedia.org/wiki/Model_release

My TFP form can be Download from:
http://www.iwannabeamodel.net/fair_tfp_form.pdf

Time For Prints Model / Photographer RELEASE FORM v2.0
Designed by Mol Smith: http:www.iwannabeamodel.net
(Helping female models move forwards)

Photographer:
Studio Name
Name:
Address:
Email:
Phone1:
Phone2:
Web Site:

Model Alias Name:
Model Real Name:
Age:
Address:
Email:
Phone 1:
Phone 2:
Web Site:

In consideration of working TFP (*time for prints and/or CD or images as digital files*) in return for posing for photographs taken by the photographer above on the date signed below at his studio in {Town} ....

We, both agree the following:-

1. Copyright of original photographs / images from the TFP shoot.
The photographer will provide me (the model) with a complete copy of the original images on CD or DVD. The photographs/images from the shoot itself are copyright of the photographer and myself independently. We are both free to do as we wish with the direct images, together with the right of reproduction

either wholly or in part, or digitally manipulated, or as composite parts of other creations and images, without needing to notify, give credit, or payment to the other party.

I understand that the photographer or myself may licence the original photo-shoot images / videos, in whole or part, independently and that any licence fee received will be retained by whichever party (the photographer, or I) licenses the images / videos to a third party. I (the model) and I (the photographer) further understand and agree that any such licences given or granted will be granted solely on a NON-EXCLUSIVE basis to ensure copyright is not lost from us to a third party.

2. Protection of my name (the model)

I agree that the above mentioned photographs and any reproductions shall be deemed to represent an imaginary person, and I further agree that the Photographer or any person authorised by or acting on his or her behalf may use the above mentioned photographs or any reproductions of them for any advertising purposes or for the purpose of illustrating any wording, and agree that no such wording shall be considered to be attributed to me personally unless I have separately consented for my name to be used.

Provided my real name is not mentioned in connection with any other statement or wording, which may be attributed to me personally, I undertake not to prosecute or institute proceedings, claims or demands against either the Photographer or his or her agents in respect of any usage of the above mentioned photographs.

3. Copyright of Art Works

I agree the photographer may use the images of me in his own art works and that such works will be solely copyright of the photographer. He/she is free to do as he wishes with these art works, together with the right of reproduction either wholly or in part or digitally manipulated without needing to notify, give credit, or payment to me. I (the model) am also free to produce my own art works from the original photos, or to produce art works from the original photo-shoot images by way of a third person. The photographer understands that any art works created by me or my agents are solely copyrighted to me (the model) and no credit or payment need be given to the photographer.

3a. The Definition of an Artwork

We appreciate that the degree of alteration and manipulation to the original photograph to form a new artwork from the photo, is, by nature, poorly defined. For the sake of clarity, an artwork is agreed to be defined as a second image where the amount of alteration is such that a minimum of 2 hours work by a proficient digital artist is carried out, and that the final image is commonly considered to be significantly different with respect to the original photograph.

4. Bonus

I (the model) will receive an electronic copy (from the photographer) of all art works produced by him/her which contains my image in part or whole, and I will be allowed to use this image in my electronic and paper portfolios without payment to him provided I honour the rest of the condition of our agreement. In addition - and upon my additional written request- the photographer will provide to me (the model) at least one free signed print from any of his artworks which includes my image in part of whole within a reasonable time of first exhibiting or selling his creation. I am not allowed to reproduce this print and have no claim other than the right of ownership of the one print itself, which I am free to sell, keep, or dispose of in any way I please. I will receive this print without needing to pay the photographer for it.

5. Agreement
I (the model) have read this model release form carefully, and fully understand its meanings and implications. I am over the age of consent (18) and state that no undue pressure has been placed on me to sign this form. I am signing here in agreement to the conditions and responsibilities on this form.

signed:_____

date:_____ (model)

The photographer will also sign below to prove his agreement with the conditions of use of the TFP images taken during this session and the rest of our agreement here.

signed: _____

date: _____ (photographer)

In plain English, this form seeks to achieve the following objectives.

TFP Objectives- Simple guide.
The TFP release form attempts to provide an agreement whereby, honour and trust are respected.:-

1. Both parties independently own the actual photos taken at the shoot.

2. They can both use these as they wish without advising the other party, except if they sell rights to an original photograph, they must ensure only **non-exclusive** rights are granted. This is to protect their own use and ownership of the photos perpetually.

3. The photographer owns sole copyright to any art works produced from the photos he manipulates or creates from material in the photograph including the image of the model herself, whole or in part. The photographer is free to license, sell, publish, exhibit, *his/her art* without payment to the model.

4. Likewise, the model owns sole copyright to any art works produced from the photos she/he (the model) or a third party, other than the original photographer, manipulates or creates from material in the photograph

including the image of the model herself, whole or in part. The model is free to license, sell, publish, exhibit, her (the model's) art without credit or payment to the photographer.

5. Any artwork produced by either party cannot be deemed to be the original unchanged photograph itself.

6. The photographer will give copies of all original photos electronically, and in the same resolution as the original, to the model without charge or fee.

7. The photographer will give a free print, signed, to the model of any art work subsequently produced by the photographer if he exhibits, sells, or licences such art work.

8. The photographer will give an electronic copy of any art works produced by him to the model, where such art works contain any element of the model so she/he can display a copy of the artwork in his/her electronic or paper portfolios.

Notes on the TF* Form
Okay. Let me walk you through each section of this form and explain it all.
Paragraph 1
You and the photographer have both worked for no pay. The objective is to end with a set of photographs of you (these days as electronic files) in his camera. Without you, he will only have pictures of the studio wall. Without him, you will look great but no-one will ever know that. He has skills and technology you don't have. You have skills he doesn't have and you travelled there. This is equal commitment to the objective. You leave the shoot with exactly the same as he leaves with: a complete copy of the images from his camera in exactly the same high resolution and image size as he has. Yours are put onto a CD, memory chip, or whatever comes next in our fast-advancing technological world. Those images are both now your copyright, and his too, independent of one-another. This paragraph of the form says you can do what you like with them and he can too—subject to the other clauses in the form. He can work on them and manipulate them and so can you, or a new agent of yours. You owe nothing to each other on this score. If you wish to credit each other—fine, but you don't have to.

You or he can sell them to a magazine or anyone else if you wish and you do not have to share out the money, nor does he! You must only ever sell rights to these photos as non-exclusive rights. This means neither you nor the photographer ever actually passes on the copyright, just a licence to reproduce the photos. You and he will always keep the copyright and you have both signed the form to that affect. If you or he wishes to share any proceeds with each other from licensing the images, great—but you are both not under any obligation to do so. I consider this is a fair and just thing. You both put something into the outcome and you can move on independently of each other and use those photos equally, as is. A lot of photographers may not like this.

Why? Because they know that every and any photograph they take is their copyright as soon as they press the camera trigger. Who do you think pressed the government to give such legal one-sided rights and ownership to the photographers? Yep! The institutions to which professional photographers belong! This paragraph in the form changes that. The photographer is signing to say that you now own the copyright too, the same as him. He has said he is okay not to be covered by *default* legislation and that he has decided to depart from his normal rights on this set of photographs taken through working with you.

Paragraph 2
This is purely to protect your privacy. As a model, you are also an actress. The way you model and the look you project, has nothing to do with your real life. You are ensuring here that if you appear say, blood-spattered, or lying draped as an adornment across the bonnet of a Porsche or Ferrari, this is not the *real* you: it is the *model* you. The photographer may use your alias name, but is not to say this is you doing this in real life! You can be credited of course as the model, but the clause here is stating that this is not a photograph of you {Miss Real Person} captured candidly at home while your man is out shopping, or whatever...

Paragraphs 3 & 4
You and the photographer have the original photos. We live in an age where pictures of people, events, and their interactions can be invented by piecing fragments together from different photos and using computers to enhance that composite image. This takes a lot of work and knowledge. If you wish to find another party to work on the photos to develop fresh images containing the element of you in the original picture, then this will no longer have anything to do with the photographer. The new image is yours outright. Likewise, if the photographer does the same, or carries out a lot of manipulation to the original photo to create a completely new art work, the new image has nothing to do with your copyright of the photos. Artwork copyright is not shared! It belongs to the creator of the fresh image!

Paragraph 5
You can't call the original photo an artwork, nor can the photographer. The photo must be substantially altered to be deemed an artwork.

Paragraph 7 & 8
You get prints and files for your portfolio of any artworks created by the photographer which include you. These are for your portfolio only and are not your copyright. The photographer owns all rights to his self-created artworks! He does not expect you to send him copies of any artworks you may create or have created through employing a digital artist to manipulate the photos from the shoot.

Improving your modelling skills

Different genres require different forms of modelling. Just turning up and running through a set of facial looks and six poses does not really make a model a professional. A great model turns up understanding the type of shots the photographer wants to do, or gets to the shoot and after discussion, understands and knows exactly how to work to make the session easy. I have worked with models with no experience and models with great experience in their specialised genre. I have worked with only a few models who could switch from one genre to another.

The better you become at understanding the requirements, the poses, the different looks and styles of the various forms of modelling, the better placed you will be to get paid work and be further recommended. For this reason, I would like to introduce you to the next section, which is my tutorial and heads up on some of the main areas of modelling. These are also the areas that I think will win you the most work. I have written the next section in a free-form style, which means I have told it the way I see it through a photographer's eye. Since it is the photographer who is most likely the paying person, s/he is the one you have to win via your modelling skills. Mixed in with this tutorial are tips and tricks to help you get the best out of your look and body shape. I also include advice regarding the more sensitive area of nudity, and some help to ensure your photographer captures what you wish to see in an image rather than what adult-image-makers might like to see! Before I begin the next chapter, I have placed an advert below regarding my

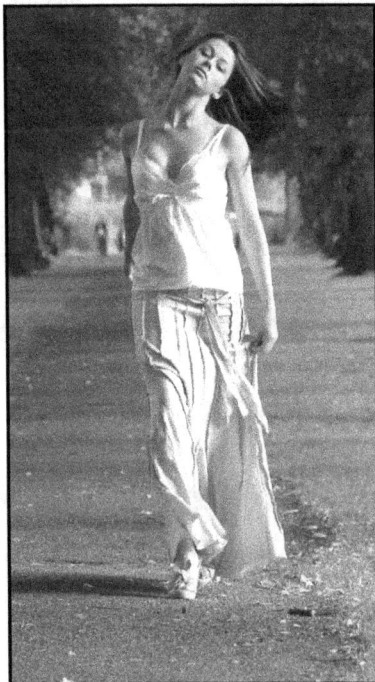

modelling portfolio creation and modelling course. This is a whole day event which you can attend here in Oxford. You will be part of a 1 to 3 people course, which helps keep your costs down. My personal tuition is assured, along with an informed photo-session, and a CD to take away, plus a five image portfolio of enhanced images and a portfolio set up on a portfolio web site for you which you can manage later. In fact, everything to get you going. The startling thing is the price!

The Model Release Form

You should only really sign a model release form if you have been paid for modelling at the photo shoot. The form releases all of your rights to the photos and any derived works from them forever. Make sure you have been paid in full before signing. If you are paid by cheque, cash it before signing. In this day and age, your face can be lifted from those image files and quite easily be transplanted onto another women's head—a woman who may be doing things a lot more explicit than you did just standing and posing for a theme you agreed to do. Most model forms do not protect against this new and novel aspect of photography in a digital age. How do you protect yourself against such exploitation? One way is to include a clause within the form itself stating you do not give permission for your face to be digitally cloned onto another model's body. This may however fix one problem but create another: maybe your body isn't great, but you have a million dollar face; a photographer may consider using your face and someone's else's body to produce 'the perfect woman'. This is quite common in advertising and some forms of art. I mix parts from different models in my own art works.

Perhaps the best way then is to include a very specific clause to protect you against unexpectedly appearing in pornographic material. Again, what is deemed pornography isn't always common to everyone, but at least we can eradicate the worst scenario. You should insert a restrictive clause into a standard model release like the one I have created here below. This will ensure you prevent a problem without stifling the photographer's sincere artistic expression of you in his work.

"I grant these rights under the condition that my face will not be cloned onto other figures or models involved with explicit sexual acts between each other, or objects, or animals".

A Simple Model Release Form

This agreement is between the following parties:

1) Studio, or Company, or Personal Name: _____ (Photographer)

Address: _____

_____

2) Real Name, or/and Alias Name: _____

(model)

Address: _____

_____

3) Photo-Session Location:_____
Time from: _____ to: _____ Date: _____

Herein - the parties above will be referred to as either Model or photographer.

The Model's statement:
I assign full copyright of the photographs taken during the session recorded above to the named Photographer, together with the right of reproduction.

I agree that the Photographer, any future licensees or assignees, can use these photographs either wholly or in part in any way and in any medium, including, but not limited to: Magazines, Books, Calendars, Internet, Portfolios, Exhibition and for Editorial or Advertising purposes.

I agree the photographs may be used to represent an imaginary person, and any associated wording will not be attributed to me personally unless my name is used. The following special restrictions will apply, provided each one is signed by both parties immediately following the restrictive clause. other than the following: (Use this area for any special agreements between the photographer and model.

Restrictive Clauses (If blank, or unsigned by both parties, there are no restrictions!):

1) {write restriction here}

      Signed (photographer):   Signed (model):

2) {write restriction here}

      Signed (photographer):   Signed (model):

I acknowledge by signing this form and, subject to any restrictions signed above, that I - the model - give up all claims of ownership, further income, editorial control and use of the resulting photographs, and any artworks derived from them. I assign all copyright ownership to the photographer and no further payment will be due. In signing, I acknowledge that I have been paid my fee in full. The photographer may assign these rights to other parties. I will not prosecute or institute proceedings, claims or demands against the Photographer or his or her agents in respect of any usage of the above mentioned photographs subject to the restrictions above. I have read this model release form carefully and fully understand its meanings and implications.

Signed:_____ Date:_____

Parent or legal guardian must also sign if the Model is under 18 year of age.

Parent/guardian:_____ Date:_____

The Photographer Statement:

I sign to agree to all statements in this form including any restrictive clauses above, I hereby state that the model has been paid her fee of _____ in full.

Signed:_____ Date:_____

Records, Accounts, Income Tax

Earning money in all western countries normally means paying tax on the income. Paid modelling is no different. If you are being paid to model part-time or full-time, then you may be liable to pay tax on the money received. The amount you are liable to pay will depend on many existing circumstances. Since most of us find it difficult filling in tax forms within a very complicated taxation system, you are strongly advised to seek out a local accountant to manage your tax affairs. In the UK, an accountant's services for you trading as a model would cost in the region of £120 to £240 pounds per year provided you do one or two things to help keep the records in good order. I suggest you get 2 file boxes. In one, you keep records of travel tickets, car running costs, telephone and internet costs, clothes and outfits you purchase along with records of all other costs you incur attending model shoots (paid and unpaid) along with paper receipts for these costs. In the other box, keep a record of cheques and cash received from any paid modelling assignments.

Any cash you receive will not show up anywhere unless you or the photographer keep records about these cash payments which are then passed to the taxman as part of his or your business records. Many people work for cash and do not declare it, knowing it is unlikely the Inland Revenue will ever know about this undeclared income! They don't tell the accountant either, as the accountant is legally bound to declare such information to the Inland Revenue. Thus, many models along with other people are receiving cash without giving receipts, knowing there is very little chance of them being caught. I must advise you though that such actions are both illegal, with very serious consequences indeed if you are caught: you would be liable for the unpaid tax, plus interest, plus additional hefty penalties for tax evasion.

There are many advantages to following the law properly, other than just maintaining a good conscience and sleeping easy without anxiety of a knock on the door. For example, if you are modelling part time trying to build a full modelling career before giving up your day job, or modelling mostly unpaid but with some paid work, you can often recover money you paid in tax earned in your full time job. You will be paying a lot of money out for your hair, make-up, outfits, communications and travel. Using part of your house or home for photo-shoots may also be considered a business cost. If your paid income for modelling is less than these total costs, you will make a loss and can claim that loss back from your PAYE tax from the Inland Revenue. So, seek out a good and competitively-priced local accountant and make sure to seek his advice about claiming your costs.

If you are receiving income from part-time or full-time modelling, you will also be liable to pay National Insurance in the UK. The amount you pay depends on your income and the accountant will advise you best about this. Also in the UK, if you start trading as a model, you are legally bound to inform the Inland Revenue as soon as possible. A £100 fine (or more) can be levied against you if you fail to tell the tax authorities within a very small time scale. It was 3 months, but this may change or have been changed by the time you read this. So check the time allowed by contacting the Inland Revenue as soon as possible.

Accountants and Accountants
Don't just pick the first accountant you find in Yellow Pages. Like other professions, accountants tend to specialise. Find one who deals with lots of very small businesses. Ask them to quote you an estimate for their yearly fee. Phone a few more and compare their prices. It is also good if they don't live too far away and they can have a 30 minute discussion with you before you agree to them doing your accounts.

You will have to fill in a tax return once a year even if you are fully employed somewhere else and on a PAYE scheme. Always be on time with your form or prepare your return online. The first time seems nightmarish but the Inland Revenue have gone a long way to simplifying the process and are extremely helpful if you contact them for advice.

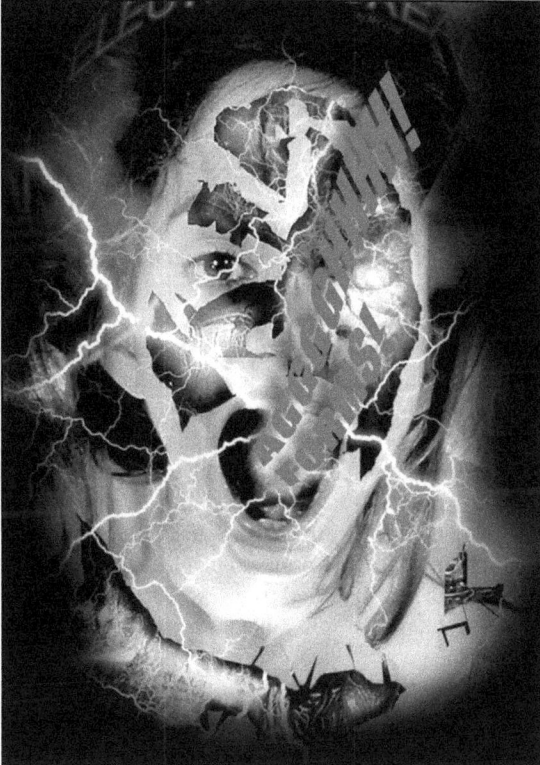

Chapter 7: How To Improve From your Start

Disappointment

Whenever one starts out on a new path, there is much to learn along the way. The first lesson is "nothing is easy!" We imagine a thing and we believe it is the way things are in practice but they rarely are. Being a model is no different in this respect to everything else we set out to do. You will have disappointments. The world is not filled with people wanting to make you a star. It is filled with a lot of people who are looking after themselves at the expense of everyone else, friendly people who sometimes don't know very much—but wish to help, and professionals who have travelled your path before you and have stuck at it.

Let's revisit your reasons for wanting to do modelling. Was it for the money? Was it for fun? Was it for fame? If you started for something fun to do, I don't think you will be disappointed. If the other reasons are true, then for certain, you are going to be disappointed unless you are prepared to work hard, have the right looks, and you can market yourself or find someone else to do that well. Remember, there are probably somewhere in the region of 400,000 females in the USA and the UK alone, trying to find fame or fortune through modelling. At any one time, this puts your odds at becoming a top model at 400,000 to 1!

Marketing yourself more!

You need to be constantly looking for photographers and artists to pay you for modelling. If you are prepared to work in a genre where a certain degree of exposure is involved (implied nude, see-through, topless), you are likely to be more successful than in other genres. Don't wait for them to find you. Get on those photographer portfolio sites and start searching for photographers and artists displaying pictures you like, and who state they pay models. Drop them a line telling them you like their work and invite them to view your portfolio.

Locate camera clubs in your area or around your state or county. They often pool funds to photograph art nude models on a regular basis. Write to them or phone them asking if they would like you to model for them. Get in contact with art colleges. They employ models on a part-time basis for life drawing classes and their rates are not bad. Ask photographers you work with either tf* or paid if you can send prints to magazines and newspapers. If you are paid and the prints get published (remember to offer *only non-exclusive* rights only), you can agree to split any money received with the photographer and make sure he/she gets credited.

Millions of clothes and goods are sold each year all over the world. Who produces the catalogues? Who is providing the models for the catalogues? Who is photographing the models? Find out. Phone and write. Get them to consider you for work. Standing still and hoping work will just drop in by itself is like hoping you bought the winning lottery ticket. Find independent clothes shops and clothes designers, not just the main-stream ones, but the people at college still waiting to break out into the world. Make contact with them. Do you party? Of course you do. Let people know you are a model. Have some model cards or business cards made and leave them in the right hands. Look at local hairdressing shops and offer to model for a style and drag a photographer you know into the process. Get your pictures in their window! Where are the exhibitions around the country? Beautiful models are a must in all avenues of exhibitions, product marketing, media promotions and many other areas. Modelling is not just confined to photography. It reaches out across all industries, hosting, event-management, celebrations, and anywhere where a beautiful woman with a great personality can make major contributions. Be a researcher and find out how these events get created and organised. Make contact. I know a woman who arranges fun casinos for wealthy clients and top companies in the UK. She regularly needs beautiful women with brains and personality to work as croupiers and hosts at those events. Get on the net. Locate the event management businesses, big and small, and send them your details saying you are looking for part time work helping as hosts and helpers at those events. And what better way to mix with clients and discretely find more people wanting your unique skills?

Your own web site
Having your own web site can be a boon too. Myspace, Facebook, and all the other social networking sites are great places to get started, but now you are a professional, having your own web site tells the world you are a serious working model. Many photographers and digital artists (em.. that's me folks), are also quite techie and many of them know how to get a web site up and running. Why not trade with one of them: you give them a few free modelling sessions and they build you a web site in return.

If you don't like that idea, many internet hosting sites now give you easy tools to build your own professional site with easy to understand tools. Don't spend hundreds of pounds having one built. Always look for ways to conserve your money and get things done by using know-how and technology already in place and proven to work. I did a quick search on Google and filtered through about 30 hosting services. These three look good for starters. I quite liked the 3rd one in the list: it's fast, ideal for models (use the photographer or gallery design), and cheap!

http://www.bravenet.com/   FREE
http://www.uk2.net/web-hosting/   Low Cost
http://www.quickonthenet.com/   For galleries, models, photographers

Once you have your very own web site, link it in to your portfolio site so when people search through and find you on the photographer and portfolio sites, they can click on a link and go to your very own site. Create a rates page and booking timetable so they know which dates you are free.

Chapter 8: Posing Course

Genres

This posing and modelling chapter covers the following genres and aspects of modelling. For most female models, these avenues are where you can build a properly paid income using the Internet and without paying out money to third parties such as managers and agents.

- Glamour
- Alternative
- Artist's Model
- See through
- Topless
- Implied Nude
- Art Nude
- Fetish

Models wishing only to appear in fashion, casual, parts, catalogue, and less risqué imagery should also read this chapter as it offers further help with posture, expressions, and stance. I have not presented this in any particular order so you can just browse through, flip pages, and learn from the examples and notes. Some of the content here will also assist models interested in acting as the dividing line between contemporary art images (advertising, film story-boarding, graphic novels) and movie/video images is increasingly becoming blurred as each channel feeds off of the other!

EXPRESSIONS

Forget about your body for a moment and consider how people react to emotional content and daily life. The way a person reacts to the external world is mostly seen through the tiny changes in their face. We learn as babies to interpret the external world most aptly—not through sound—but through what we see. Our world depends initially on other people: our mums. So begins the real form of communication, aided later by speech and language. Throughout the world there is one common, invisible dialect. It is the way our faces talk (reveals) our every thought and intention despite our adult methods used to disguise them. Actors spend many hours practicing their expressions. Good communicators observe people to see the tiny inflections in their facial muscles. In any image of a human being, we are naturally drawn to the face to get our clues as to what is going on. Looking at a camera and doing nothing, except looking like you are thinking about looking at the camera, is about the worst expression any model can do. At all times, a model is not looking at the camera: she is looking at the imagined people looking at her (or the final picture of her) or else she must not be looking at the camera at all. In the latter, she is observed—and her expression must be a reaction to her thoughts and interactions with the world that the viewer will peer at in the future. So, the model is not at the shoot, she is creating a piece of the future—the photograph or art image, which will ultimately be seen by her viewers and observers.

Apprehension. Surprise. Mild Fear

In these pictures above, Jenny expresses a set of emotions based on mild apprehension and fear. Her eyes look away towards the unseen thing causing her concern. They are wide, almost in disbelief at the terrible thing in their view. She tilts her head back in 3 of the images as if unconsciously recoiling away from the threat. Only 1 image, the first one in the set, shows her ducking behind her shoulder as if to cower in paralysed terror. Notice how the stark lighting enhances the moment of surprise that she is experiencing, and how her mouth is open, how her breast expands with a sudden intake of air. Now you look in the mirror and practice this. Look at movies with an objective eye and see how the characters respond to different threats. What do their bodies do? How are they expressing fear, surprise, shock, and anxiety in their faces and posture? Do they bring their hands up and reel backwards like Jenny does here?

Glamour poses are the ones you more often see in certain newspapers and magazines. Jenny does the expressions and the poses well. Lifting your hair up creates boldness, screaming simulates dynamic emotion (Orgasm? Anger? Excitement?). All these photos are untouched. They came out of the camera exactly as you see here. Messy hair gives the impression of being in contact with someone or having been in action. Compare the photos here with those on the opposite page, where Jenny is producing a different set of glamour and pin-up looks.

GLAMOUR

Lips slightly parted, looking straight into the lens of the camera, Jenny smoulders! Here is a soft provocative challenge to the observer. You have to over-do glamour pose expressions a bit to make them work. Have a go in front of a mirror.

More glamour and sexy pose expressions. The large photo in the background shows Jenny looking away from the camera. Her lips are slightly pursed. There is a slight look of vulnerability here which contrasts with the freedom and inhibition imbued to her through her hair being blown by a large fan.

In the bottom photo on the opposite page, Jenny has her eyes almost closed. It is as if she is saying "I am too good for you!"

Eyes half-closed and staring straight at you, Jenny is challenging you, searching you (the observer) as if to see if you are a match for her personality and beauty.

OH! And that is what you say if you want to look cheeky and like you're teasing the observer.

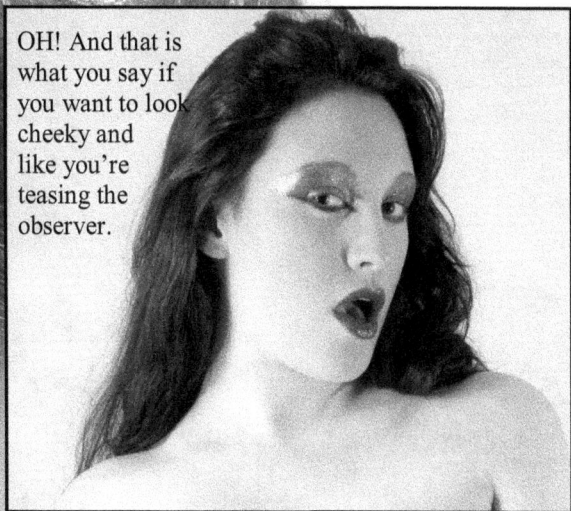

Disdain? Jenny shrugs away. Arrogance is displayed as if she has judged you to be not worth her time. She is beyond your reach.

More GLAMOUR

Study these expressions carefully. Understand why they work and practice them yourself so you can do them as well as Jenny.

Sunglasses make a great prop. Look at how many different expressions Jenny does here. Look at each one and question what the expression is conveying to you. What aspects of her face and head are most involved with change?

6

7

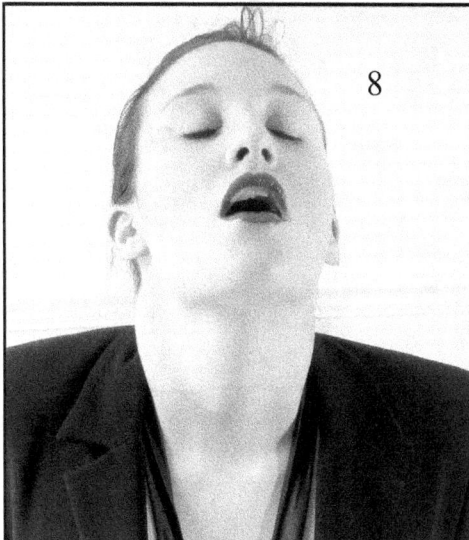

8

1)   Looking over the
     sunglasses with a
     slight look of disdain.
2)   Pleasure.
3)   Making decisions.
4)   Pouting whilst playing
     with clothes.
5)   Sideways 'fancy-you'
     glance.
6)   Pouting and cross.
7)   Vulnerable.
8)   Bliss.

Also pay attention to Jenny's head position. How she places it, looking up or down, tilted, etc. even just a little bit greatly enhances and enforces her expression.

Her stance in each photo is also important, although it is not visible in this set.

GLAMOUR POSES

Glamour is all about showing off glamorous women. This means posing to get the best currently-perceived body shape to be manifested. Less clothes and semi-nakedness, if done well, enhances many glamour images. Glamour evolved from the Pin-up style images of the 40's and 50's.

Your stance and posture need to change according to the camera position and its angle to your body. See the two photographs below. Which one do you think is better than the other? The answer is the one on the right is good and the left one is rubbish. In the first image, Jenny leans back (A) from the camera and also to the right (B). The camera is very low and her leaning away foreshortens the top part of her body. The camera's low view point amplifies this. In the second image, Jenny has straightened (D), dropped her head forward slightly towards the camera, and the camera has been raised in line with her hip.

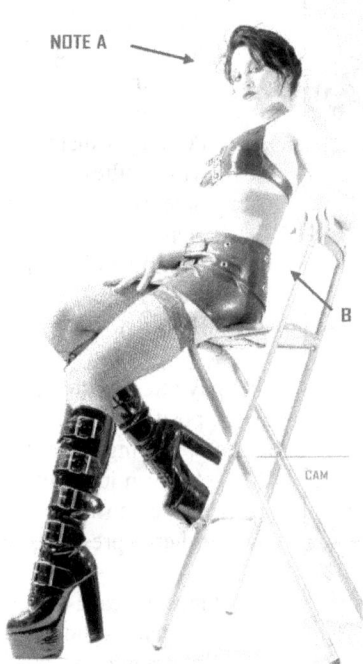

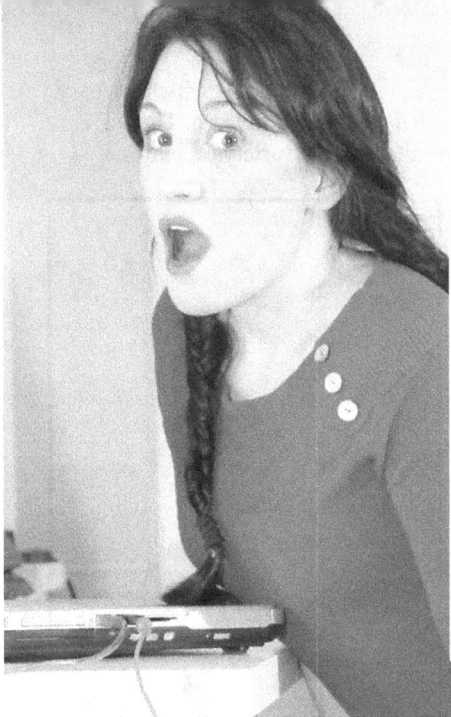

Spicing up the image

A little voyeurism spices up glamour images. In the large image and top right inset, jenny feigns surprise at being caught with her legs clumsily placed. She quickly hides any taboo exposure. Notice how she has deliberately positioned her legs awkwardly as if she lacks maturity. The bottom inset provides an image of her just before we, the observers, pop into the photo. She is intent on her 'student' work and thus not paying attention to her position and revealing pose. This is all acted to provide a cheeky degree of titillation, much like those seaside postcards of a bygone era.

A few pages of poses which are easy
to do and quick to learn. These are
suitable for a variety of genres.

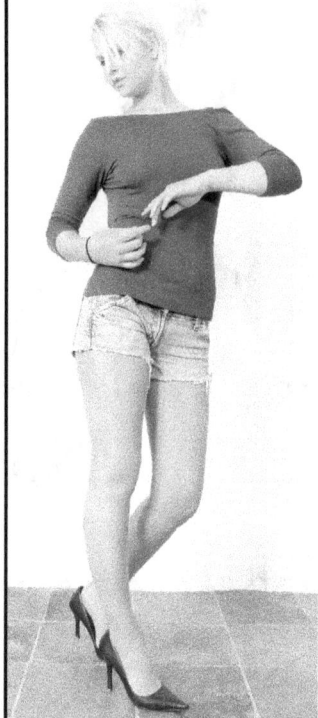

Some Standard Poses

The poses on these two pages have a positive effect on your posture. They increase curves and improve shape in small and subtle ways. You should study the relationship between arms, shoulders, head, legs, and feet. Invisible lines at certain angles are being repeated by the model's pose. I have put some guide lines in this first image to demonstrate!

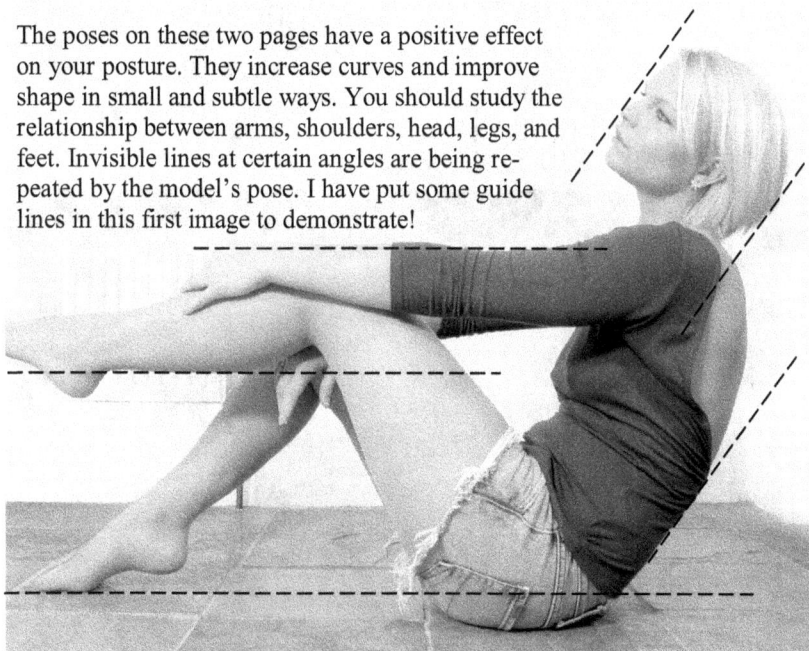

Implied Nude
Wins Paid Work

Some of the best implied nude poses mimic the public's perception of classical nudes from old paintings. Notice here how the model has hidden her nipples, pubic bone, pubic hairs, and vaginal line with just her arms, which themselves look naturally positioned.

This model's angle to the camera hides her
pubic area, while her arms hide her nipples.

Implied nude model
work provides one of
the best opportunities
for paid work. Many
artists working non-
commercially are quite
happy to pay 20.00 to
40.00 pounds an hour
for a model with a
good physique and
pretty face.

The two images below
Are also implied nude.
See how the models
are hiding their more
sensitive areas?

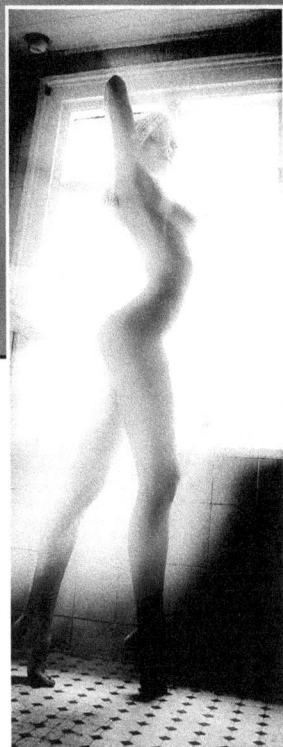

Posing for different lighting systems

Photographers generally use up to 4 different lighting systems: daylight, flash, constant light (video lights), and tungsten lighting. Posing for flash lighting is the easiest. Although you should remain fairly still during the actual moment the camera is clicked, if you forget—the short period of the flash duration will do a good job of freezing you in the image. Tungsten light may appear bright to your eyes but is not so bright to the camera. The photographer shoots at slower speeds. This means that when he clicks the camera button, the camera shutter stays open slightly longer than for flash. Any movement by you when the shutter is open will blur the image. So stay very still and hold your breath when being lit with tungsten lighting. Daylight and video-lighting will demand various degrees of stillness from you according to which effect the photographer is trying to achieve. Listen out for his direction and instructions in these cases.

Learn to hold your breath just before the camera click. Breathing out slowly is also effective. Try not to blink as the photographer takes the shot, and do not stare directly at any of the main lights or you will not being to see much for a while afterwards. Pay attention to where your hair and arms are as you may inadvertently have them in a position which blocks light to your face, causimg ugly shadows to darken your skin and hide important detail.

Many models find it difficult to know what to do with their hands and arms. If in doubt, try placing your hands against the top of your thighs, on your hips, behind you, behind your head, or on your head. Make sure the sides of your arms are placed to leave a gap between the sides of your body and the sides of your arms so the narrowing of your waist and your body shape is not spoilt.

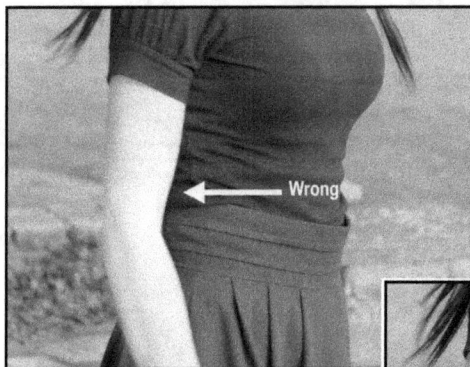

Look at the two pictures here. Which one shows the narrowing waist? See how it improves the shape of the model's body compared to the other image?

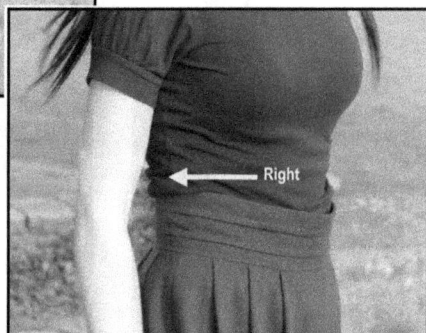

"Leave a gap between your waist and your arms to improve body shape!"

Chapter 9: Inspiration

The Good. the bad, and the beautiful

We are coming to a close and I thought I would round up my advice to you to leave you with something positive. First of all, I have stressed throughout this book about safety, and how difficult it can be to find paid work unless you are prepared to model with a degree of nudity. I have also advised you of the incredible number of females currently offering modelling services via internet portfolio services. This may put many of you off. For all that though, appearing in superior images, currently being created, may give rise to a degree of mortality. The art world remains 20 to 50 years behind new trends and emerging art forms. The last decade has witnessed the rise of the digital artist and the internet-presenting model. It has also created an unprecedented opportunity for collaboration between model and artist (a photographer is also an artist) to create contemporary images never seen before throughout history. I have been part of this revolution which still continues to expand and grow stronger as I write. Ultimately, at some point in the future, this period of New Art will become recognised, written about, debated over, and the pioneering art from this era which has stood the test of time will be sought after.

By becoming a model right now, you may also become the woman to look out from a million places in the future, much like DaVinci's Mona Lisa has dominated our view of enigmatic women in the past. Few things in life, other than having children, or sadly—murdering tens of people—are likely to offer you the lottery ticket of fame on a grand and monumental scale, as modelling today for contemporary image makers. Photographers and artists publishing their works (I do) will guarantee their images survive long after their deaths. A copy of every published book has to be placed in the British Library, who have to preserve it and make sure the data in the book is safely carried into the future—art books included. Find photographers and artists who publish their work or who have their work published by third parties. Appear in their best and most revolutionary, provocative, or evocative images, and your children may one day be finding you the new Madonna and a universal icon in a future society.

Of all the pursuits we do in life, the act of creation at any level is the most important one. Being part of an artistic adventure may not keep the bills paid or lead to a startling and rich career, but it will fill your spare moments with an addictive set of experiences unlike any other. On these grounds alone, I would like to inspire you to take part and try modelling if only to be able to turn a page of a book and find yourself there—the focal point and star of an incredible and beautiful picture… just like the females will do when they turn this page now and discover what I have created with them through their modelling with me.

Mol

Eve models to help pay her way through university, but she also models because she adores beautiful and powerful art. So, in the cold month of December, she duly undressed, put on a very see-through netted dress, walked out into our garden and transformed herself into a winged angel coming to earth and touching mortal soil for the first time.

The inset below shows the raw shot straight from the camera. The large picture to the right is what was eventually created from that photo. Eve will forever be able to look at the 200 year light-fast print, and whatever befalls her in the future, know she exists in the exotic world of human imagination.

Autumn

Index

Jargon Buster

Chaperone	Companion / Friend / Minder
Digital Artist	Expert Image Creator across many platforms & media
DPI	Dots per inch (image resolution) 300dpi for prints/72 for web
JPG	Compressed Image Format
MUA	Make Up artist
Photoshop	Professional Image Editor (software from Adobe)
Port	Portfolio
Portfolio	Set of photographs
Shoot	Photographic Session
TF*	Time for {something}
TFP	Time for Print
TFCD	Time for CD
TIF	Non-compressed Image Format (Save a copy as a Tif always!)
Tog	Term for a photographer

scent of a woman

* 9 7 8 0 9 5 5 7 1 3 7 1 2 *